PRAISE FOR *BODY CALM*

'Body Calm *guides you, in the most gentle grounding way,
in how to let go of all that disturbs your body, mind and
spirit, and bask in the healing energy of now. Every body
needs* Body Calm. *I recommend it with all my heart.'*
SONIA CHOQUETTE, NEW YORK TIMES BESTSELLER OF *THE ANSWER IS SIMPLE*

'Body Calm *is a great follow-up to* Mind Calm. *Sandy
presents another dynamic, creative, insightful and practical
guide to being fully alive and present in your own life.'*
ROBERT HOLDEN PHD, AUTHOR OF *HAPPINESS NOW!*

'There is nothing more powerful and life-changing than daring
to be fully embodied. Everything becomes possible with our
presence. In Body Calm, Sandy Newbigging has given us a
sacred, practical roadmap that leads us back into our bodies
and back into the awareness of the healing forces we all contain.'
MEGGAN WATTERSON, AUTHOR OF *REVEAL* AND
HOW TO LOVE YOURSELF (AND SOMETIMES OTHER PEOPLE)

'I have seen in tens of thousands of people worldwide how
stress make us sick. In Body Calm, Sandy addresses many
of the challenges that I've frequently seen causing disease,
including uncomfortable emotions, unhealthy beliefs
and an unforgiven past. He shares elegant and effective
meditation tools that help take the body out of stress and
into a healing state. It's an approach that can be used on its
own or alongside other healing modalities, and one that I
highly recommend to anyone on a journey of self-healing.'
KARL DAWSON, CREATOR OF MATRIX REIMPRINTING

'Sandy shares insights and wisdom about how the mind and
body connect, and teaches us powerful tools for reducing the
effects of stress on our bodies. This is a very healing book!'
DAVID R. HAMILTON PHD, AUTHOR OF *HOW YOUR MIND
CAN HEAL YOUR BODY* AND *I HEART ME*

'All of the spiritual and personal development under the sun
is useless if we are unable to embody it. In Body Calm, Sandy
effortlessly guides us to create a harmonious relationship
with the one home we have been given for this lifetime – our
physical body. I wholeheartedly recommend this book.'
REBECCA CAMPBELL, AUTHOR OF *LIGHT IS THE NEW BLACK*

D1079757

'I was curious how Sandy would combine his years of helping others heal from chronic illness, with his skills as a world-class meditation teacher. The results are outstanding. Body Calm not only shows readers how to move out of stress and into healing, but also enables them to get to the emotional causes of their health conditions and transform them. This is yet another masterpiece from Sandy and a book that everyone recovering from an illness or disease should own and utilize.'
SASHA ALLENBY, CO-AUTHOR OF *MATRIX REIMPRINTING USING EFT*

'Sandy has written an important book. In today's modern, digital, fast-paced society, you may seldom give attention to the messages coming from your own body. And yet your body is the seat of much wisdom and self-understanding. In this fascinating, creative and comprehensive book, you're offered excellent ways to begin calming and healing yourself.'
SHAMASH ALIDINA, AUTHOR OF *THE MINDFUL WAY THROUGH STRESS*

'This beautiful book is a real gift to anyone wishing to use their mind–body connection to aid their healing journey. It provides a powerful and effective set of meditative tools that are easy to use and give you the keys to wellness.'
PHIL PARKER, CREATOR OF THE LIGHTNING PROCESS®

'I was lucky enough to have meditation taught to me personally by Sandy, which was enlightening. Body Calm is equally powerful, written with such in-depth precision, clarity and insight and it helps you to understand why illness occurs within the body. I have studied many types of meditation but Sandy's CALM techniques have enabled me to achieve a lightness, a calmer mind, a relief from stress and to find harmony.'
SADIE FROST, ACTOR, PRODUCER AND BESTSELLING AUTHOR OF *NOURISH*

'By coming into your body, being with what is and allowing yourself to experience it instead of changing it, healing takes place. In Body Calm, Sandy Newbigging teaches you how to do just this. His techniques are practical and straightforward and his explanations clear and understandable. Body Calm is a great book to support your healing journey.'
ABBY WYNNE, AUTHOR OF *ENERGY HEALING*

'I enjoyed reading Body Calm so much that I'm going to read it again. While moving through the pages I found that my body wants to LIVE this book – and I'm sure your body will too.'
RICHARD FLOOK, AUTHOR OF *WHY AM I SICK?*

'Body Calm *is a wonderfully uplifting book that reminds us the body is the home of our soul. Sandy has dedicated his entire life to helping people find a sense of peace and stillness within – and he helps us recognize that these qualities are indeed possible. Sandy is a walking demonstration of peace. This book invites you to step up with integrity to do "the work" in order to reach a state of healing with your body. If you are ready to move beyond the limitations of your fears for health, this book is for you!'*
KYLE GRAY, AUTHOR OF *ANGEL PRAYERS* & *WINGS OF FORGIVENESS*

'Sandy embodies peace and he wants to share it with you and the world. Although we live in a fast-paced world, full of external stressors, we can master how we react to them. Body Calm *gives you the tools to do just that, so if you want to experience emotional freedom and create harmony in your body and life, read this book and transform.'*
JOSEPH CLOUGH, AUTHOR OF *BE YOUR POTENTIAL*

'Body Calm *is full of easy-to-use techniques that bring calm and healing to your body. Your body is more than a tool by which you move through life; it is intelligent. Through Sandy's tools you can tap into that somatic intelligence and regain your health and happiness.'*
BECKY WALSH, AUTHOR OF *YOU DO KNOW*

'These are the times for people to take authority into their own hands, mentally and physically, and Body Calm *is an extremely efficient tool to do it. Thank you, Sandy, I loved it and will recommend it to anybody who wants to heal.'*
TIM VAN DER VLIET, AUTHOR OF *SPIRITUAL AWAKENING*

'Body Calm *teaches us how to listen and tune in to our body wisdom and discover the emotional causes of our health issues so we can work with our body to heal. Sandy has written an inspiring book full of delicious insight and awesome meditative tools to make the process simple yet powerful.'*
CHRISTY FERGUSSON PhD, AUTHOR OF *HOT, HEALTHY, HAPPY*

'With our modern tendency to live disconnected from the needs of the body, Sandy's book offers an accessible and eloquent way to drop beneath all the mind chatter into happy and easeful living.'
CHARLOTTE WATTS, AUTHOR OF *THE DE-STRESS EFFECT*

'Sandy is a man on a mission to bring deep calm to our crazy, stressful lives. In this wonderfully accessible book he offers the tools we need to both calm down and wake up... which is the secret to living a happy, healthy, creative, fulfilling life.'
TIM FREKE, AUTHOR OF *THE MYSTERY EXPERIENCE*

CLIENT TESTIMONIALS

'I would recommend everybody use Body Calm. Sandy's techniques have enriched my life beyond words.'
G. BRIGHT, UK

'Body Calm has the potential to create a shift, not only in respect of health, but crucially also in respect of human consciousness.'
A. HENRY, UK

'Body Calm has really helped to calm my body! I feel better in my own skin than I have ever felt. I particular like the Embodying Exercise and have been using it with amazing results.'
F. CANTER, UK

'It is so important to see the mind–body connection and how emotions affect health. Sandy is an expert teacher and presents the information in an accessible way that inspires.'
D. McBRIDE, USA

'Alongside conventional medicine, Body Calm provides a self-help strategy for optimum health. Sandy has a wonderful way of revealing things that will turn light bulbs on – in rooms inside yourself you never knew you had!'
Y. SAVAGE, UK

'If you want to experience a sense of peace and calm, regardless of your health, then Body Calm is for you. It's empowering.'
N. FORDER, UK

'Sandy integrates ancient and current methods and science and makes it all so practical. I love the Body Calm Meditation technique and would recommend everyone use it.'
C. BEATY, UK

'The most obvious sign of Body Calm's impact on my health was when I went to my doctor for 24hr-blood pressure monitoring. In the past my blood pressure has always been raised. However to my amazement it was normal when using Body Calm.'
M. CARRINGTON, UK

'Body Calm is an excellent follow-on from Mind Calm or to do on its own. Sandy is a knowledgeable and inspiring teacher who always gives much more than you could ever wish for.'
K. MAY, UK

'Body Calm is an excellent system, so full of essential information while also being really practical and engaging. I feel better already!'
A. PARKER, UK

BODY CALM

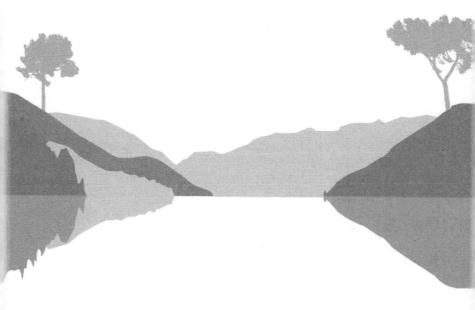

BODY CALM

The Powerful Meditation Technique
That Helps Your Body Heal
and Stay Healthy

SANDY C. NEWBIGGING

HAY HOUSE

Carlsbad, California • New York City • London • Sydney
Johannesburg • Vancouver • Hong Kong • New Delhi

First published and distributed in the United Kingdom by:
Hay House UK Ltd, Astley House, 33 Notting Hill Gate, London W11 3JQ
Tel: +44 (0)20 3675 2450; Fax: +44 (0)20 3675 2451;
www.hayhouse.co.uk

Published and distributed in the United States of America by:
Hay House Inc., PO Box 5100, Carlsbad, CA 92018-5100
Tel: (1) 760 431 7695 or (800) 654 5126
Fax: (1) 760 431 6948 or (800) 650 5115; www.hayhouse.com

Published and distributed in Australia by:
Hay House Australia Ltd, 18/36 Ralph St, Alexandria NSW 2015
Tel: (61) 2 9669 4299; Fax: (61) 2 9669 4144; www.hayhouse.com.au

Published and distributed in the Republic of South Africa by:
Hay House SA (Pty) Ltd, PO Box 990, Witkoppen 2068
info@hayhouse.co.za; www.hayhouse.co.za

Published and distributed in India by:
Hay House Publishers India, Muskaan Complex, Plot No.3, B-2,
Vasant Kunj, New Delhi 110 070
Tel: (91) 11 4176 1620; Fax: (91) 11 4176 1630; www.hayhouse.co.in

Distributed in Canada by:
Raincoast Books, 2440 Viking Way, Richmond, B.C. V6V 1N2
Tel: (1) 604 448 7100; Fax: (1) 604 270 7161; www.raincoast.com

Text © Sandy C. Newbigging, 2015

The moral rights of the author have been asserted.

The information given in this book should not be treated as a substitute
for professional medical advice; always consult a medical practitioner.
Any use of information in this book is at the reader's discretion and
risk. Neither the author nor the publisher can be held responsible for
any loss, claim or damage arising out of the use, or misuse, of the
suggestions made, the failure to take medical advice or for any material
on third party websites.

A catalogue record for this book is available from the British Library.

ISBN: 978-1-78180-560-2

Printed and bound by CPI Group (UK) Ltd, Croydon, CR0 4YY

To every body.

CONTENTS

PART II: HARMONY HEALS

Contents

ACKNOWLEDGEMENTS

I would like to thank the Hay House team who believe in my message and me, including Michelle Pilley, Amy Kiberd, Jo Burgess, Julie Oughton and Diane Hill in the UK office and Reid Tracy and Louise Hay in the US. At Hay House, I would also like to thank Tom Cole, Ruth Tewkesbury and Jessica Gibson for everything you do to help my books reach the hands and hearts of the readers. In addition I would like to thank my excellent editor Sandy Draper for the improvements you made during the edit.

I've bounced my ideas for this book off many beautiful people. I'm grateful to Kyle Gray, David Hamilton, Sonia Choquette and Robert Holden for your pearls of wisdom, and to Jennifer Countryman, Calum Murray, Richard Abbot, Sasha Allenby, Bryce Redford, Lesley Weston and Laura Jones for your encouragement, interest and passion. You guys rock, big time!

I'm grateful to the universe for guiding me to the USA to meet and work with Peter Blake, who gave his guidance on the philosophy, directories and Embodying Exercise. Your commitment to awareness and selfless giving is inspiring and your advice has been invaluable.

I would also like to thank my family for their unconditional love and every single person who's attended one of my clinics, courses or retreats – including the growing clan of Mind Calm and Body Calm coaches. Without you all, this book would not have been possible.

And finally, infinite gratitude, as always, goes to my spiritual teacher, MKI, for bringing me home to the beating heart of stillness. I feel very blessed.

Rest is best + Harmony heals

Introduction

HELPING YOUR BODY TO HEAL

'Go home and get some rest.' Visit a doctor, work with a health practitioner or seek advice from a friend and one of the most common recommendations you'll receive if feeling unwell is to give your body rest. It seems an easy enough task. Relax. Take some time off, put your feet up and chill out so your body has a better chance to heal. Despite 'get some rest' appearing to be a simple thing to do on the surface, most people I meet don't know how to calm down, disengage from doing and let their body 'be'.

> *This inability to stop stressing stems from a number of subtle sources that we are going to uncover and resolve with Body Calm.*

One of the main causes of stress is our habit of excessive thinking. The interconnection between the mind and body is scientifically proven, and so our physical form is constantly responding to and experiencing what we are thinking about and feeling. This means if you go home to rest but take your busy mind with you, then your body won't necessarily end up getting much respite at all. Yes, you may physically lie down in your cosy bed or on your comfortable couch, but if your mind keeps mulling things over at a million miles per hour, you will very often find that healing is hindered and your physical conditions continue.

Body Calm gives your body the rest it needs to recover.

STOP STRESSING START RESTING

Scientists and doctors agree stress is harmful to health. Stress has been found to lower the immune system, trigger inflammation and increase blood pressure. It plays a key role in cardiovascular disease and digestion disorders, speeds up the growth and spreading of certain cancers, and interferes with sleep leading to chronic fatigue and insomnia. More heart attacks happen at 9 a.m. on Monday mornings than at any other time of the week, with many experts citing the stress associated with having to face another week at work being the potential cause of the 'Monday cardiac phenomenon'. The list of stress-related physical symptoms and conditions goes on and all point to the fundamental conclusion that getting your stress levels under control can be quite literally life-saving.

Stress, by far, is the biggest preventable cause of the majority of physical diseases and premature deaths on the planet. At the same time, meditation is known to be the most effective cure available for significantly reducing stress. Yet, despite these facts staring us in the face there are still relatively few methods of meditation used to actively support the healing of the body, with even fewer techniques having been specially designed to target the mind-based causes of stress and ill health.

With Body Calm, I want to bring
meditation and healing together as the ideal
marriage made for health heaven.

You don't need a doctorate from Cambridge or Harvard to know your mind is constantly causing changes to occur within your body. Simply watch a movie that's a bit of a tearjerker and the undeniable evidence of the mind–body connection can fast end up rolling down your face. Bear witness to injustices and you can feel your blood boil. Your stomach can churn when contemplating concerning thoughts and you can find your mouth watering at the mere thought of a food you enjoy. Yet, again, despite the proof being prolific, it is easy to neglect the mind when helping the body to heal and stay fit and healthy.

Dependency on doctors and drugs

We live in a world that relies upon doctors and drugs to try to fix the body: 70 per cent of Americans take at least one prescription drug while more than half of the population take two. In the UK, in 2014, 50 per cent of women and 43 per cent of men regularly took prescription drugs, with more than a fifth of men and nearly a quarter of women taking at least three prescribed medicines.[1] The UK's National Health Service gave out a massive 22 million prescriptions for paracetamol alone, a 13 per cent rise on 2013 and at a cost to the taxpayer of over £80 million.[2] Global spend on prescription drugs is expected to reach $1.3 trillion as soon as 2018. Over one billion prescriptions were given out in England in 2014[3] with four billion written in the USA in 2011. Based on these figures, some alarming trends are very evident: our dependency on doctors and drugs are moving in an unprecedented upward direction.

Growing up, if ever there were any early signs of sickness, my first stop was the doctor's surgery to pick up a prescription and be advised to go home and get some rest. I believe the consequence of this conditioning is an unhealthy dependency on doctors and a sense of powerlessness to properly heal without pharmaceuticals.

It wasn't until I got into holistic health myself that my mind-set started to change. Especially after accidentally creating a form of therapy called Mind Detox that went on to be used globally to heal the mind-based causes of physical, emotional and life problems. Then, with the introduction of meditation into my daily routine, I began to appreciate a part of the doctor's advice that I'd previously taken for granted – 'go home and get some rest'. To this day it's hard to say what has been more impactful: the pills and potions or the peace that's come from taking time out to relax and recuperate. Perhaps both. All I know is I cannot remember the last time I turned to a pharmaceutical drug. If ever I do end up feeling under the weather, I've noticed it takes around the same amount of time to feel 100 per cent again, if not quicker, by simply meditating as often as possible while my body does its healing work.

Incidentally, I'm not suggesting that you toss your prescriptions in the bin and never open your medicine cabinet again. However, I *am* saying that until you start using meditation to reduce your stress levels and get good quality rest, it's hard to fully grasp the big benefits that both can have on the physical functioning, recovery rates and wellness of your body.

Body Calm aims to 'help' the body to heal.
I am not saying you should never call on
doctors or drugs ever again and ONLY use
Body Calm but rather, if you need to heal or
want to stay healthy, then it is wise to adopt
an integrative strategy that includes modern
medicine, alternative methods and meditation.

The insights and exercises shared in *Body Calm* have come about during the past decade through thousands of hours of personal meditation and the experience gained from working with thousands of individuals from around the world at my clinics, academy courses and residential retreats. My clinical practice has given me the opportunity to meet and treat people presenting almost every physical condition you can name, from acne to arthritis and headaches to hyperhidrosis. I've worked with a multitude of people on a wide range of conditions to discover and resolve the potential mind-based causes. When undergoing my meditation teacher training, I went away to meditate day and night for many months, sometimes up to 18 hours per day, and have gone on to attend month-long meditation retreats since, to further deepen my personal practice. On top of that, I've run health and meditation retreats at some of the world's best resorts in UK, Turkey and Thailand and trained coaches in my methods from more than 15 countries. Overall, I believe it is the unique combination of my extensive therapeutic work, academy training courses and the many months I've dedicated solely to meditation that have allowed me to create Body Calm and write about how to help the body heal and stay healthy.

Using the techniques I'm going to share, you will learn how to stop stressing and be calm. You will heal the common causes of stress-induced 'dis-ease' and return to a more restful state that is highly conducive for self-healing and optimum health. Sound good? Well, the benefits of Body Calm extend way beyond the return to rest – and begin with a rather curious question.

HOW DO YOU KNOW YOU HAVE A BODY?

Inquire as to how you know you have a body and you will probably conclude that you know because you can see and feel it. In other words, you are aware of having one. This rather obvious recognition means that within you now exists something that is aware of your physical body. With Body Calm you are encouraged to become interested in, and attentive to, the conscious awareness that is aware of your body – as you engage in any self-healing activities to fix, change or improve your health. In doing so, Body Calm can give you a new relationship with your physical form. By getting to know your real Self, beyond your body, you will make the inner shift required to stop being in a battle with your body, and to instead enjoy the kind of calm coexistence that allows health and peek physical functioning to flourish.

Vast quantities of vital healing energy are wasted when you fight against your physical form.

When you are in harmony with your body, you ramp up your energy reserves and dramatically increase your inborn self-healing capabilities. Having a healthy relationship with your body requires you to know and experience that, although you *have* a body, you are *not* your body (I will explain this more in Chapter 11). It also requires you to change your relationship with your mind and body by being more consciously aware.

A meditation technique for 'peace with body'

Most of the suffering that happens when a person is ill originates in the mind. Yes, conditions can be physically uncomfortable. But they become mentally stressful and cause emotional anguish when we start thinking about them. As a result, being at peace with the body begins by getting a peaceful mind. By reducing the time spent thinking, you rest in to the aspect of your Self that is aware of the mind and body. Naturally, as you engage less in negative thinking about your particular condition, you learn to peacefully live with your body.

In my experience and observations, by far the best way to befriend your body is to rediscover your real Self. When I refer to your 'real Self' I'm talking about the permanent and unchanging part of you that has been present since before the day your body was born; the conscious awareness that is not only aware of your body, but also your thoughts, emotions and everything else that happens during your daily life, too. Being consciously aware, you discover that you benefit from effortlessly experiencing the peaceful presence of your being.

Remarkably, you can come to notice that your awareness never gets sick, doesn't malfunction, go faulty and is free from pain or any difficulty happening within the body. To your relief and delight, you can reconnect with an on-going inner state of restful calm that is perfect, whole, and completely untouched and unconcerned by any temporary physical problem. With this all-important shift in perspective, you benefit from what I call 'peace with body', whereby you remain calm even if your body happens to be going through a tough time. 'Peace with body' means you don't need to suffer if you have a physical problem. You also no longer need to postpone feeling better until your body gets better because being aware of your real Self feels great.

TOP TIP: HOLISTIC HARMONY = HEALTH

Stress is the result of there being disharmony within your mind, body, soul and life. By clearing the causes of inner conflict while learning to rest within the aspect of your Self that is always still and never gets sick, you can regain the holistic harmony required for your return to radiant health. With less stress to deal with, your body is able to more easily and effectively undertake its repair and maintenance projects. In fact, most of the exercises in this book are to be done from a consciously aware perspective, instead of from your thinking mind. So as you proceed, I urge you to explore the calm of your own consciousness.

ABOUT THE BOOK AND TECHNIQUES

If you are feeling unwell then it is safe to assume you want to get on the road to recovery as soon as possible. Consequently, this book reflects this by setting the scene in Part I with the life-changing philosophy at the heart of this self-healing system, before immediately diving into the Body Calm meditation technique.

The meditation technique is a daily practice that brings about greater mind calm and physical rest. It has been specially designed to give you a healthier mind-set that promotes better health. By using it regularly to be more consciously aware you'll enjoy two immediate benefits:

1. By being less caught up in your busy mind, your body gets the rest it needs to recover

2. By being present and aware, you naturally begin to relate to life in a more harmonious and stress-free way.

To help your body rest and recover even faster, Part II reveals the seven secret sources of stress and offers 'shifts in awareness' and quick-start cures for cultivating more holistic harmony. Once you've been meditating for a while and started to adopt the habit of being consciously aware, Part III will then show you how to find calm with the Embodying Exercise, which can be used anytime you need to heal a physical condition or when you encounter stressful experiences in your life. The Embodying Exercise works by clearing inner conflict and enhancing positive traits. In doing so, it also brings about greater harmony within your mind, body, soul and circumstances, which is the precursor to health and happiness.

Part III also includes five comprehensive directories listing the mind-based causes of issues relating to your body parts, organs, five senses, 12 systems of the body and 101 physical conditions. Used alongside the Embodying Exercise, which you'll find in

Chapter 14, this will give you the chance to discover and resolve the possible mind-based causes of your physical concerns. Used as a whole, Body Calm offers a system of self-healing that brings resolution to the often hidden causes of compromised health, while helping you to live in a harmonious and happier way.

GO HOME AND REST IN YOUR REAL SELF

Central to Body Calm is the invitation to rest in your conscious awareness. As you progress through the book and play with the teachings and techniques shared, I invite you to notice when you are experiencing a sense of inner stillness or silence. When you do, you can be confident in these moments that you are being your real Self. I like to refer to this conscious awareness as the 'Infinite and Eternal I' (or 'infinite and eternal eye', if it makes more sense to you). Consciousness has no outer edges, is always present and beyond the physical body. It is a serene and secure state of being to return to, where all is wonderfully well and calm is continuous. It is my hope that by being your real Self, the phrase 'go home and get some rest' takes on an entirely new meaning for you and that once you return, you stay for good.

Go home to the heart of your real Self and rest in the haven of calm that is your consciousness.

Part I

REST IS BEST

Chapter 1

BODY CALM PHILOSOPHY

Health is much more than the mere absence of disease. It is a state of holistic harmony that enables you to meet your individual needs while actively pursing your life purpose. The Body Calm philosophy has the power to transform your relationship with life and make you healthier and happier. By living by it, your everyday experiences will become extra enjoyable and meaningful, your stress levels will drop significantly, and you will be more able to actively help your body to heal and stay healthy. Beyond the likely body benefits, your career, relationships, wealth and wellbeing can also be positively impacted. Quite simply, I cannot overstate the profound and positive paybacks that can come your way if you apply it.

For the biggest returns from this philosophy, however, don't take my word for it. Instead, actively apply it to your own life and see what happens. It won't work if it remains a collection of intellectual ideas to think about. Rather it is an experiential way of relating to yourself and your life. Let the proof of the philosophy's validity come from how your health, happiness, satisfaction and life success improve. Do your best to refrain from jumping to judgements or rejecting any aspect before you've regularly used it. The reality is if your current beliefs and attitudes were 100 per cent working in your best interest, there's a chance you wouldn't have the physical condition(s) that motivated you to buy this book! This is not to say any physical conditions are your fault, rather that you have a golden opportunity to question your assumptions and be open to alternative ways of relating to your mind, body, soul and life situations. Remain open and then, as you engage with this empowered and enlightened way of living, you may find it to be a defining moment. Ready? Let's explore the philosophy now.

HEALTH REFLECTS YOUR RELATIONSHIP WITH LIFE

The purpose of your life is to live fully and completely. Although this might seem like a rather simplistic or understated purpose, it is profound. Most people aren't living fully or letting life experiences come to their conscious completions. All too often, people resist what happens and thus stop situations from fulfilling their positive purposes. They also don't experience life in its fullness because they are so preoccupied by their mind-made version of reality instead. Busy recalling the past, distracted from the present or focused on thoughts about the future, they miss the magnificent moment and the magic that is constantly unfolding. Tragically, countless people only ever tentatively exist. With the intention of 'getting by', they never get around to living fully and end up dying unaware of their remarkable Self and the awe-inspiring beauty and perfection of life.

The purpose of your life is to live: engaging every experience as a sacred invitation to be present and rediscover more of your radiant real Self.

Everything happens to help you to fulfil this purpose. You are perpetually presented with invitations to move from stress to serenity, ignorance to awareness, separation to oneness, and in doing so, learning how to live more fully and completely, never wasting a moment. As a natural consequence, life is less about *what* you do and more about who and how you are, *as* you do; less about what happens and more about how you engage and respond to whatever occurs. Do you resist or rejoice? Do you fight life or use everything to learn how to be more flexible and free? Do you act the victim or welcome the gifts you are given to grow? The choice can be yours, as long as you know that life happens not to hinder, but help you.

Knowing this ultimately means *what* you experience is less important than your relationship with life. With the right attitude, you can use *all* that happens, including ill health and adversity, as invitations to step up, wake up and show up fully. Reclaim your power to peacefully progress towards your purpose and be the most wise and wonderful version of your Self.

HEALTH IS THE BY-PRODUCT OF HOLISTIC HARMONY

Although it can sometimes feel as though life has something against you and is trying to put you down, the reality is the complete opposite. Every moment, you are given the events and experiences that are exactly what you need to be elevated into the fulfilment of your life purpose. Again, I appreciate it may not always feel this way, especially when life is particularly challenging. However, if you take this principle on board, then I promise your life will take on a deeper meaning. You will see the sacredness of situations and will suffer far less from what happens.

Fighting against life events that don't fit your hopes or expectations takes its energetic toll and creates conflict. Over time, the resultant disharmony is stressful for the mind and body, causing *dis*-ease, ill health and unhappiness. So instead of feeling attacked by life, I invite you to assume that everything happens to help you live fully and completely.

*With this attitude, you can move mountains and heal
the un-healable due to the harmony that occurs within
your heart, mind, body, soul and circumstances.*

Stress is a symptom too

Stress is often named as the main cause of ill health. However, in my opinion, it isn't the *ultimate* reason why people get sick because stress is caused by conflict. Furthermore, for conflict to be present within your mind, body or life, there exists the presence of the two opposing forces of resistance and attachment. By this I mean, whenever you encounter a stressful situation, it is not the event that makes you stressed. Instead, it is the disharmony arising from an inner conflict between a reactive resistance to something you don't want and an unseen attachment to something you think you need. Within the context of reducing harmful forms of stress, Body Calm aims to heal these hidden causes of conflict.

*Stress is a symptom of there being a conflict between
what your mind wants and what your soul knows
you need; for you to fulfil your life purpose.*

Recognizing stress is caused by the inner push-pull conflict of resistance and attachment can be an extremely empowering revelation. It stops you being a victim to circumstance and puts the power to be calm, and thus help your body be healthy, firmly in your own hands. This is vital because you may not be able to control life to make it *always* pleasing and pleasant. However, when you notice you're stressed, you can take simple steps to actively reduce resistance and appease attachment, returning yourself to a more restful state.

For example, let's say you are suffering emotionally from a relationship split to the point it's affecting your health. For it to be stressful means there's an inner conflict. You may be resisting being alone and have an attachment to keeping the security that the relationship provided. In this case, you would be resisting 'being alone' and the attachment would be to 'security'. Until you become aware of the inner conflict and become at peace with it, the stress, emotional suffering and physical conditions brought on by the break-up, will most likely continue. Being willing to make this inner shift gives you holistic harmony and makes for a healthier and happier life. It is the secret to stopping stress from making you sick and, as we progress, you'll find many examples and exercises to help you harness the power of harmony and aid physical healing.

> *Health is the natural by-product of having harmony within your heart, mind, body, soul and life.*

Although the finer details of the resistance and attachment are unique to your situation, the principle remains the same. If there is conflict, and therefore unhealthy stress and disharmony, the opposing interplay of resistance and attachment will be happening. More generally, as long as you continue to be in conflict with life by forcing it to fit your expectations, then you will stay stressed. This in turn causes your body to exist within a state of prolonged *dis*-ease and lead to the loss of optimum health. But if you are willing to live out this philosophy, then I promise you a more stress-free and serene life that allows for true health to flourish.

An energy-boosting bonus from this philosophy

The forces of resistance and attachment cause energy to flow outward and away from physical healing. It takes energy to constantly be pulling or pushing at life. Over time, if you live in an ongoing state of conflict, you will find your energy levels become depleted, along with your ability to heal and stay healthy. On the other hand, when you are consciously aware of your real Self and using everything that happens to help you, you automatically allow energy to remain strong and build up within your body. The more energy you have, the better your health.

Resistance and attachment = Energy out.
Body calm and embodiment = Energy in.

LIFE INVITES YOU TO EMBODY MORE OF YOUR SELF

If everything happens to help you to fulfil your life purpose of living fully and completely, including experiences such as family politics, job uncertainly and financial constraints, then resisting and remaining attached slows your progress towards becoming the person that life is inviting you to be. Within the context of the Body Calm philosophy, and in the case of the relationship example above, its ending is an invitation to cultivate an inner sense of security because it doesn't serve you to stay in any relationship where the foundations are based on fear. It is not your purpose to remain scared of losing someone or be needy of security, and so life can lead you through a break-up to help you embody what real love is and experience relationships that are free from fear.

Harmony is restored when the conflict is cleared.

When there is harmony, there is less stress and the body is better able to function properly. With Body Calm, healing happens through embodying certain positive virtue(s) that fulfil the purpose of the situations in life that you've found stressful. These include appealing qualities like connection, strength, peace, love, truth, clarity, compassion, contentment, forgiveness and so on. Such virtues are the qualities you need to *be* in order to no longer resist or be attached and therefore experience harmony within yourself and life. Embodying the virtues is part of your purpose because they allow life to serve its conscious-raising purposes so that you may live fully and completely.

Embodying the virtues also brings completion to events or experiences that may have been unresolved because the purpose of them happening has finally been fulfilled. Instead of staying stuck at the difficult parts of your path, embodying the virtues allows you to use all that happens to serve a positive purpose. This means if you have anything in your life causing you stress, discomfort or negative emotions, and therefore potentially harming your health, you can be sure that they simply remain incomplete. Nothing happens to hurt or hinder you or make you sick. Everything happens to help you to fulfil your purpose of embodying the positive qualities that will set you free from stress and return you to your real Self. Once you've embodied the traits that the events were given to teach you, the conflict collapses, they move to completion and no longer cause stress.

Spiritual teachers have said: 'You are what you seek', meaning if you want peace or love or strength, for example, then you already are these virtuous states.

Now I appreciate that this may not appear to be the case, especially if you aren't currently feeling peaceful, loved, strong, etc. However, I believe these teachers were not referring to your mind-based identity of who you think you are, but instead to the consciousness of your real Self. When you rest in your real Self (with the techniques I will share), you become aligned with, and gain access to, the positive virtues that will make life more harmonious, your body healthier and your mind happier.

I like to think about it this way. Imagine you have a personal i-cloud of positive virtues, similar to the online storage service operated by Apple Inc. and within it exists the virtues of love, peace, compassion, confidence, etc. During your day-to-day life, a range of events and experiences occur to encourage you to 'download' the relevant virtues into your mind and body. You are asked to do a presentation at work to gain more confidence or to experience relationship challenges with a loved-one so that you may embody more compassion.

Clearly, this idea of having your own 'virtuous i-cloud' is a rather light-hearted analogy to explain my point. But if you play with the philosophy – that life happens to help you to embody the positive virtues that you need to be – then you'll end up using everything that happens to live more fully and completely and thus enjoy a great life. With Body Calm, we will explore the parts of your life that remain incomplete and bring them to completion, for your healthier and highest good.

EASIER TO GO WITH THE FLOW THAN FIGHT

Although it may sound complicated, please don't overthink it or get bogged down by any specific details. The Body Calm philosophy boils down to a handful of principles that are easier to apply than not. This is because they work in accordance *with* the natural tendencies of your mind, body and life, rather than *against* them. Chances are, you've been stressed (and potentially ended up sick) because you've been working against the natural flow and order of things. But, as it is easier to go with the flow than fight, adopting the Body Calm philosophy can be much easier than you may think.

Rest is best and harmony heals.

Live by this simple philosophy and you will see your stress levels subside substantially and your health and happiness soar. Sound good? To get started, let's explore the benefits of meditation, which is by far the most powerful way to get some much-needed rest.

SUMMARY: BODY CALM PHILOSOPHY

- The purpose of life is to live fully and completely.

- Everything happens to help you to fulfil your purpose.

- What you experience in life is less important than your relationship with it.

- Health is the natural by-product of having harmony within your heart, mind, body, soul and life.

- Disharmony is stressful for the body and causes *dis*-ease.

- Stress is a symptom of inner conflict between what your mind wants and what your soul knows you need.

- Conflict continues when there is the unseen push-pull of the opposing forces of resistance and attachment.

- Ill health is an invitation to heal the areas of your life in which you are not living fully and completely.

- Harmony happens when the conflict is cleared.

- Life is inviting you to embody more of your Self.

- You have access to a personal 'virtuous i-cloud'.

- 'Downloading' the virtues helps you to step up, wake up and show up fully as the most wise and wonderful version of your Self.

- Healing happens through being your consciously aware real Self and embodying the positive virtue(s) that fulfil the purpose of your life events and experiences.

Chapter 2

BIG BENEFITS OF BODY CALM

Meditation techniques like Body Calm, which stimulate the relaxation response, have been used by countless cultures from around the world for centuries. The relaxation response is known to decrease physiological stress and psychological distress. Over the past few years there have been thousands of scientific studies published on the effects of meditation on physical health, with significant benefits being proven in relation to anti-aging, pain relief, combating and coping with cancer, and improvements for insomnia sufferers.

HEALTH BENEFITS OF MEDITATION

The positive payback from adopting a regular meditation practice is compelling. I want you to be in no doubt as to why you don't just want to, but *need* to meditate, if being healthy is important to you. Here you'll find a selection of my favourite research studies and some additional benefits, so that your motivation to meditate is strong and steadfast.

Body benefit 1: Slow aging and live longer

One study conducted by the University of California during a three-month meditation retreat found that there was an increase in telomerase activity in meditators.[1] Telomerase is the enzyme that maintains and builds telomeres, which affect how your cells age. These tiny caps on the DNA help to stop it unravelling and research shows longer telomeres help to protect us from disease. Quite remarkably, the study found that meditation could slow the aging process of cells. The implications of this are massive because if the telomeres stay healthy, your cells are more able to stay healthy, your body stays healthy and you can literally live longer.

By using meditation to calm down you can potentially slow down aging and even live longer.

Staying with the anti-aging benefits of meditation, other research has found meditating regularly can even offset the age-related thinning of the prefrontal cortex of the brain, which suggests that meditating helps parts of your brain stay healthier longer.[2] Furthermore, in another fascinating study, researchers compared gene expression in meditators versus non-meditators over an eight-week period. Incredibly, meditation was found to impact 1,561 genes in novice meditators and 2,209 genes in experienced meditators.[3] These findings are so significant because upon closer scrutiny of the genes that were impacted in the meditators, they were ones associated with slowing the rate of cellular decay. Again, this suggests that meditation can slow aging.

Body benefit 2: Pain relief without painkillers

Recent research has also shown that meditation inhibits and relieves pain perception, with some studies finding that meditation reduces pain-related neural activity in the anterior cingulate cortex, insula, secondary somatosensory cortex and thalamus.[4] Other research reports meditation helps in overall pain management. These findings are not only encouraging for people experiencing prolonged pain but also support the feedback I've received from my chronic pain patients. I've observed chronic pain being a symptom of blocked energy due to unresolved and resisted life events where people have been unable to express themselves fully. Through regular meditation, there appears to be an increased willingness to 'speak their truth'. Also, by learning to focus on the present moment, many have reported pain reducing and, in some cases, completely disappearing. I believe this is because pain is one of the ways the body moves your focus towards aspects of your physical form that require attention. When you become able to direct your attention in a focused manner and then place it upon the area of the discomfort (without thinking about it), the pain has served its purpose of flagging it to your attention. If you have chronic pain, I encourage you to explore this for yourself.

Meet Nikki, who no longer needs morphine

Nikki had a brainstem stroke 15 years ago, aged 31. The trauma left her with chronic pain from occipital headaches, nerve damage to her neck (where the artery dissected), numbness and post-central nerve pain radiating down her left side and into her foot. The medical profession referred to her as a 'complex case'. Over the years she tried a cocktail of medication and was so desperate that she took whatever the specialists suggested. However, nothing worked and she experienced many negative side effects.

The last option she was given by her consultant was brain surgery in the form of deep brain stimulation, which she was obviously reluctant to experience, as it's a high-risk procedure. On many occasions she attempted to wean herself off the drugs, but would go through hell during the withdrawal process and then only last a week or two before her willpower gave way and the pain would flare up tenfold. This led to her taking even more drugs, including up to 90mg of morphine daily. After years of suffering Nikki was dejected, had no lust for life and felt useless, weak and scared.

That is until she began using Body Calm. Within three months of using it, she reported moving from surviving to thriving by meditating every day to help her body heal. Today she is morphine free and no longer needs blood pressure medication. As an added benefit, she's also sleeping through the night for the first time in years.

Helping headaches and migraines

Chronic tension-type headaches (CCTH) are the most common type of headache and stress is widely known to be a major trigger. In one study examining the effect of meditation on headaches, it was found that the severity, frequency and duration of CCTH were significantly different in regular meditators compared to non-meditators.[5] Overall, people who meditated were found to benefit from early relief in chronic tension headaches. In addition, recent research coming out of Wake Forest School of Medicine in the USA explored how meditative stress-reductive techniques can have an impact on migraines.[6] Again, it was found that headaches were less severe and the duration was shorter.

These findings mirror what I've seen in the migraine sufferers I've helped over the years. Often due to literally having 'things on their mind', they've reported that using meditation to let go of overthinking and remain calm amid crises has led to a decrease in their physical symptoms – with some clients never getting migraines again. Often the key was finding peace with unforgiven past events using similar methods to those outlined in Chapter 9.

Body benefit 3: Combat and cope with cancer

It is common for those facing a cancer diagnosis to feel both scared and somewhat helpless as to what they can do to help the body heal – beyond that of traditional medical interventions. In a recent study by the University of Calgary, Dr Linda Carlson led a team of scientists in exploring the effects of meditation and group therapy on breast cancer patients.[7] The study compared the telomeres of patients doing regular meditation and group therapy sessions versus patients who only attended a six-hour stress-management seminar, which represented standard treatment. While the scientists found that telomeres shortened in the control group who only did the single seminar, very encouragingly, they didn't shorten in the group who did meditation and group therapy. This shows that meditation and being open about your feelings can have a positive effect at the cellular level in women with breast cancer. Furthermore, this is just one study that helps to prove the importance of meditating regularly and being willing to feel and express your emotions if you want to actively help the cells of your body to remain fit and healthy.

Meditation has also been found to help premenopausal women diagnosed with breast cancer in a study conducted by the University of California.[8] It was found that the women undergoing a six-week meditation programme had significant reductions in both perceived stress levels and inflammatory signalling, along with reduced fatigue and sleep disturbance. In another study, 117 cancer survivors went through an 11-week meditation programme to determine the impact on cancer-related symptoms.[9] Quite remarkably, significant improvements were found relating to fatigue, pain, insomnia, constipation, anxiety and depression in the people who meditated. Furthermore, it was also noted that the interpretation of illness as some kind of punishment also decreased significantly. Overall, it established that the people who meditated over the sustained period of time reported improved satisfaction and coping styles. Although I'm not suggesting that meditation can cure cancer, the research points towards regular meditation being a powerful way to aid healing and I would always recommend it is used as part of an integrative approach.

Body benefit 4: Sleep without counting sheep

Insomnia is experienced by millions of people worldwide. Not only can it be frustrating to be unable to get to sleep but, due to a lack of good quality rest, insomnia can lead to a whole host of physical conditions because the body is given little opportunity to do its maintenance and repair projects. In one study by the University of Southern California, it was found that across two groups, the people who meditated showed improvements in sleep quality compared to the control group who didn't meditate.[10]

In another randomized controlled trial of meditation and chronic insomnia, 45 individuals were asked to meditate over an eight-week period.[11] The results again showed that the ones who meditated reported significantly greater reductions in 'Time Awake Time' and 'Insomnia Severity' when compared to the control group who didn't meditate.

These studies and others confirm what I have observed teaching meditation. Time after time, individuals who've found it difficult to sleep have reported enjoying the best sleep they've had in years. In my experience, it also appears that meditation helps you to enter sleep at a deeper level and get better quality rest from the sleep you get. Whereas normally it takes around five hours to eventually enter the deepest levels of sleep, if you meditate, your body is resting before entering sleep and once you drift off, you may quickly experience and benefit from the deeper realms of rest.

TOP TIP: MEDITATE YOURSELF TO SLEEP

One of the reasons many people find it hard to sleep is because they can't switch off from thinking. The longer you lie awake not sleeping, the more concerned you can become about how tired you might be the next day. However, if you meditate yourself to sleep using Body Calm, you won't engage in so much worrisome thinking and so you'll find it easier to fall fast asleep when your body and mind are ready. Not only that, but knowing your body gets ample rest from meditation, you can change your relationship with sleep. Believe it or not, you may even find you are happy to have the opportunity to get a few extra hours of meditation in, rather than sleep, before the next day.

Body Benefit 5: The silent solution to stress

In January 2015, researchers from Dallas, USA, said that meditation-based practices were found to support women with traumatic stress.[12] Highlighting it gave the opportunity to develop heightened awareness and focus on the present moment. Their research explored how meditation may perpetuate human resilience for women who have experienced trauma and found that meditation helped them to accept what's happened and 'use silence instead of speech as a healing modality'. Personally, I find this research very exciting because it supports a major premise of Body Calm: namely, that instead of thinking at length and using talking therapy to stop feeling so upset or stressed about life, meditation offers a way to be at peace with past and present moments by experiencing the inner stillness and silence of conscious awareness. I've seen countless cases of the big benefits of letting go and being still, even amid challenging circumstances. Not only can it lead to more resilience, it can support the healing of the body due to reduced anxiety and enhanced acceptance of 'what is'.

Imagine a bathtub with a shower over it. During your daily life, the water is flowing, filling the bathtub. In this analogy, the bath is your body–mind and the water is stress. Without meditation, the water (stress) fills the bathtub (your body–mind) and before too long can end up overflowing – leading to emotional unease and physical conditions. However, with Body Calm, you have a way to pull the plug on this problematic predicament. Closed-eye Body Calm meditation is the equivalent of removing the plug and draining the accumulated water (stress) and open-eye Body Calm meditation reduces the inward flow of stress. The more you meditate, the more you become like Teflon® to stressful situations, with it no longer sticking to your body or mind. As you can imagine, the combination of closed and open-eyed Body Calm meditation can offer a superb solution to living with less stress.

Body benefit 6: Healthier and happier hearts

Numerous studies have also explored how meditation can help lower blood pressure. In a recent systematic review and meta-analysis of 12 studies involving 996 participants,[13] it was found that people who meditated had reductions in systolic and diastolic blood pressure. Again, this is reflective of what I've observed in my practice. People with high blood pressure tend to present with feelings of overwhelm and through meditation have felt more capable of dealing with day-to-day life.

Staying with the heart, chest pain from coronary heart disease accounts for more than eight million emergency department visits every year in the USA alone. In one review study by the Tulane University School of Medicine in New Orleans, researchers examined the multiple studies conducted over the past decade regarding the effects of meditation on various aspects of cardiovascular (CV) risk factors.[14] It was reported that meditation had been shown to improve conditions such as hypertension, type 2 diabetes mellitus, dyslipidaemia, high cortisol levels and even decrease CV mortality.

*Using meditation to be calm and love life
more can make your heart healthier.*

Millions still to benefit from meditation

In the scientific community, stress is regarded as having a profound impact on quality of life, with meditation often being cited as an effective treatment for stress-related diseases. Meditation is known to improve the health of the cells due to the beneficial cellular membrane changes that come about from the parasympathetic response that occurs when meditating.[15]

Meditation has been shown to significantly reduce perceived stress, sleep disturbances and symptoms severity in fibromyalgia patients.[16] It's been found to help people with Multiple Sclerosis (MS) through improved quality of life and enhanced coping skills,[17] with one study finding meditation helps people suffering from MS with regard to depression, fatigue, disability levels, relapse rates and the over activity of the disease, in a large international sample.[17] Understandably, this will encourage the 100,000 people with MS in the UK alone, but millions of others still stand to benefit from starting to meditate because the health benefits for many other health conditions have also been found to be significant and far-reaching. This is especially apparent when you consider that studies have reported increases in the immune system levels in meditators compared to people who don't meditate.[18]

*All together, with the majority of research published
in recent years pointing to big physical benefits
from adopting a regular meditation practice,
it isn't a matter of if you might benefit, but
realizing all the ways that you will benefit.*

BENEFITS BEYOND THE BODY

Body Calm can also give you non-health related benefits. In my years of teaching meditation, I have yet to meet a single person who hasn't ended up better off from meditating regularly. Here are some of the most common benefits:

Life benefit 1: Calm and contentment

Feeling uneasy, anxious and discontented are the natural side effects of excessive thinking. If you are caught up in judgemental thoughts, then you will inevitably feel your negative thinking. By using Body Calm to stop thinking, you feel your awareness instead. Due to consciousness being still, quiet and inherently calm, when you are consciously aware, that is how you will feel. Also, as we'll discuss more in Chapter 10, discontentment is the by-product of believing the present moment not to be enough. Thinking leads to comparing your current moment to either a better past or a hopefully improved future. However, as you fill your attention with the present moment, you will find there is fullness right now. You can still have goals for the future, but moving towards them with your attention firmly rooted in the present moment allows you to enjoy every step of the journey.

Life benefit 2: Unconditional confidence

Thinking too much can also lead to low confidence. If you are relying on the voice in your head to tell you how confident you can feel in any given situation, then your confidence will depend largely on your beliefs and past experiences. If you've picked up self-limiting beliefs along the way and had things happen that have knocked your confidence, then you will carry these old opinions and feelings about your capabilities into your present day. However, when you use Body Calm to change your relationship with the voice in your head (which is also just a series of opinionated thoughts), then your mind will no longer dictate things so much. You will be free to embrace new ways of being and doing, and engage in life with an unconditional confidence.

When I was younger, I was petrified of public speaking and was also told that I had dyslexia. At school, I faked illness for months to avoid going because I couldn't face reading aloud in English class. However, having changed my relationship with my mind (which you will begin doing in Chapter 3), I continue on my journey irrespective. These days, I often speak in front of large groups, sometimes consisting of hundreds of people, and with the publication of *Body Calm* I am now the author of 10 books. I'm not saying this to blow my own trumpet, but to impress upon you that Mind and Body Calm can allow you to follow your heart in more courageous ways.

Life benefit 3: Loving relationships

The less you judge the more you love. It is as simple as that. The mind needs reasons and requirements to deem people, places, events and things as loveable. However, when you let go of the thinking mind, there remains no reason *not* to love. Furthermore, you also find it much easier to love yourself, too. As is the case with confidence, if you are going to rely on the voice in your head to tell you that you are lovable, then you might be waiting a very long time. You risk never living up to the high standards of your mind. Even if your mind does say you are loveable, this can end up being an ego-based love that is not as pure as the love that resides within the heart of your awareness.

Meditation can help you to rediscover your own being. Beyond all the doing, your being is the foundational landscape within which every thought, feeling and action takes place. Quite beautifully, you can discover that your being is an all-encompassing presence of unconditional love. You've never, for one iota of a second, been separate from love, as it's lived within you since before your body was born. With this recognition, you get to 'live in love', which is to spend your days inwardly aware of the presence of love. Fear falls away in your relationships because love can no longer be taken away from you and you are free to love with an open heart.

Life benefit 4: Present-moment living

Every thought you have is about the past or the future, even the ones you are having about what's happening now. The moment has to happen before the mind can commentate on it. Therefore, if you want to be present, you must be willing and able to let go of the thinking mind. The great news is meditation provides the perfect platform to practise being present. You can use Body Calm meditation anytime you notice that you've been thinking and, with practice and a little gentle perseverance, you can cultivate the habit of living aware of now. Instead of thinking about a past that is forever gone or future possibilities that may never happen, you get to live in reality, instead of a mind-made time-based version that only exists in your head. Naturally, you rarely dwell on sadness, shame, guilt, regret or any other emotions that require the past to be justified. Similarly, feelings of fear and anxiety about the future can fade away, leaving you fully here to marvel in the magnificent moment.

Life benefit 5: Perform at your best

Being distracted by the thinking mind is a major cause of underperformance. When you are thinking you are no longer completely focused on the task in hand. Instead, you are thinking about what you are doing and/or what needs to be done later. In the process you can open yourself up to letting your mind limit your potential.

Your best work flows when you are still
within the movement of life.

However, when you are consciously aware, you enter into the optimum state for performing at your best. You discover that you are much more capable and creative than you may have thought. Spontaneously, ideas come to you that you've never considered before and you get much more done with far less time and effort. Perhaps, ironically, you can find that by stopping occasionally throughout your day to meditate, you can end up much more productive and successful in all you do.

Life benefit 6: Get to know your real Self

You are not your mind, body or life circumstances, as they are all temporary and in a constant state of flux. You are the permanently present consciousness that has been the underlying, still, silent, contextual setting through which all transient human experiences move. I believe knowing and experiencing 'Who You Are' is the primary purpose for which we are born. Every experience is an opportunity to get to know your real Self better and the more you do, the more joyful you become. Although there are many ways to get to know your Self, meditation is one of the most effective and proven modalities, as it can help you to disengage from *doing*, to return to your beautiful *being*.

Life benefit 7: Freedom for life

Living freely, you don't need to control your thoughts and emotions or your external events as much, if at all. Your sense of self, emotional wellbeing and life satisfaction are no longer determined by the content of your mind, the state of your body or what happens. You experience life as perfect, whole and complete, and every event as a fascinating invitation to embody the most awake version of your Self. Naturally you notice that the more you need to control everything, the less free you end up being, whereas, when you are at peace with 'what is', you are liberated from limitations and enjoy freedom for life.

YOUR MOTIVATION TO MEDITATE

Having explored the potential big benefits of Body Calm, which of them stand out as your must haves? To get motivated to meditate and keep doing it long enough to build the momentum you need to cause physical changes, it is vital that you get super clear on why you ultimately want to do it. So before proceeding please take a moment to answer this key question:

What do I want more than anything else?

Knowing what you want can help you to save a huge amount of time and effort, which, in turn, helps you to avoid adopting ineffective strategies that stand in your way of attaining it. Now, if you're reading this book there's a big chance that healing a physical condition may come high in your list of priorities. If you want to heal yourself then great, I recommend you go for it wholeheartedly. However, it is also wise to aim deeper than purely physical changes. To do this, consider:

What would perfect health give me?

Answering this question is so important because your heart's highest hope is intrinsically linked with your health goals. By that I mean, your body will be more able to heal when you are experiencing harmonious states of being like peace, love, joy and contentment. You want to be careful not to fall into the trap of answering this question about *what* with a *how*. For example, it is common for people to say they 'want' to be less anxious, to change their career, to not be in physical pain or to be able to do what they want. Although these answers are all well and good, they aren't what your heart ultimately wants. Instead, they are how your mind believes what your heart wants is possible. What will you feel with no more anxiety? What will changing your job give you? What will living without pain be like? For what ultimate purpose do you want to be able to do what you want?

You will know you've found your 'what' because it will be an inner emotional state or experience and using the Body Calm philosophy and techniques, you can enjoy it far quicker than you may think possible. What you want exists within your conscious awareness; and is experienced by *being* your real Self. It is the by-product of no longer letting your head get in the way, of disengaging the dogmatic doing and stopping all the stressing, by instead resting in the oasis of calm within your inner consciousness.

Amazingly, you can discover that your heart's highest hope goes hand in hand with healing. By embodying it with the help of Body Calm you can positively impact your physical health and overall wellbeing. I highly recommend keeping your personal motivations to meditate at the forefront of your intentions as you continue with your Body Calm journey.

Scientists have proven the healing effects of meditation and the millions of meditators from around the world are testimony to the boundless benefits possible. Now it's your turn to prove it for yourself as it's time to learn how to enjoy Body Calm!

SUMMARY: BIG BENEFITS OF BODY CALM

By meditating regularly, you can:

- Slow aging and live longer.

- Relieve pain without painkillers.

- Cope with and support the healing of cancer.

- Get to sleep without counting sheep.

- Significantly reduce stress.

- Have a healthier and happier heart.

- Boost your immune system.

- Feel more calm, contentment and confidence.

- Love in an unconditional way.

- Live in the present moment.

- Perform at your best.

- Get to know your real and reliable Self.

Chapter 3

STOP STRESSING, START RESTING

Body Calm and better health begins with a calmer mind. The mind–body connection means that if you are constantly caught up in your busy mind, it is near impossible to experience a rested body. When it comes to the interplay between your mind and body, the body exists to help the mind do its work and without the mind the body cannot fulfil its function. They are designed to work in harmonious unison and support the fulfilment of your life purpose. However, if you are stuck in a cycle of stressful thinking, then your body's ability to remain balanced and perform optimally can inevitably end up compromised. To help the body to heal, it therefore pays dividends to make it a priority to cultivate mind calm.

In this chapter, I introduce why you want to think less and reveal step one of Body Calm meditation so that you can get on the restful road of recovery and radiant health.

UNCONSCIOUS THINKING TO CONSCIOUS CALM

When I wrote *Mind Calm*, the introduction began with the question: *How do you know you have a mind?* The answer was: *You know you have a mind because you are aware of it.* Mind Calm is possible because you are not your mind. Instead, you are the consciousness that is aware of your mind.

To understand what I mean by this, imagine being outside on a clear day, looking up at the blue sky. Fully focused on the big sky you find yourself feeling relaxed. Then out of the blue a bird flies across your field of vision. Noticing the bird, your focus moves away from the sky and becomes placed upon the bird. But you don't stop there; as you then start thinking about the bird – wondering what type of bird it is, where it's going and why it's flying solo. Before you know it you're caught up in your mind, feeling concerned about whether the bird is lost or has somehow ended up separated from its friends. In doing so, you stop feeling as relaxed as you once did when you were just aware of the sky. You are now feeling your concerned thinking.

What have the sky and birds got to do with mind calm?

Within you now there exists a big sky of calm, conscious awareness, with thoughts (birds) flying around within it. If you've been feeling stressed and not getting good quality rest, there's a very high chance you've become disconnected from your own conscious awareness and are much more focused on the thoughts happening in your mind. This is due to the fact that you feel what you focus on and your body follows the movement of your mind.

The more you think, the less rest your body gets.

Mental chaos can occur whenever you fall asleep from being consciously aware. When you stop being awake to your own awareness, you inevitably get caught up in the myriad of thoughts occurring in your mind. Preoccupied by thinking, you end up identifying with a mind-made version of yourself and life. You spend your days feeling whatever you are thinking about because your emotional state follows your mental activity. Consequently, you can find yourself on an emotional rollercoaster: up and down, positive and negative, comfortable and uncomfortable – depending on the content of the current thoughts happening. All the time, with your body following your mental and emotional escapades, you unsurprisingly create a tense inner climate that makes the likelihood of physical *dis*-ease highly likely.

LOST IN THE MEANDERING MIND

How much of your day do you spend unconsciously thinking? Research would suggest a lot! Harvard University[1] recently did a study exploring how much people think and found the average person spends 47 per cent of the day lost in the thinking mind. Almost half the day, over the years adds up to half a life! If you add on top of the 47 per cent, the amount of time you also tend to sleep during the average 24-hour day cycle, it really doesn't leave much time to be present and experience all that life has to offer. Furthermore, I believe the Harvard study gives a conservative figure, with the reality being much higher. The study required the participants to be aware enough to recognize when they were thinking. In my observations teaching meditation, most people aren't aware of how much time they spend in their mind. Recognizing when you are and aren't thinking can be very subtle and requires a relatively high level of Self-awareness to state accurately – usually attained through regular meditation.

Irrespective of the actual figures, the main point to note is that when you are thinking, your body is feeling and responding to whatever you are thinking about. This means that if you are trapped in your busy mind for much of your day, your body is put under pressure and subjected to a huge amount of unnecessary stress. Over the years this can have a negative effect on your health and happiness.

The more you think, the more your
mind will find justification to think
some more, and again, even more.

The mind makes sense of reality by judging whether life is good or bad, right or wrong, better or worse, positive or negative. More often than not, the mind judges things as bad, wrong, worse or negative. If you're not aware of the antics of the mind, then once you've unconsciously judged something as problematic, you will find yourself feeling compelled to think. You will either start thinking about possible solutions, drop into a 'poor me' story around why life's unfair, or in attempt to at least be positive, consider some pearls of wisdom. Irrespective of your personal way to deal with perceived problems, you will often end up thinking about ways to improve your predicament.

This unseen habit of judgement and then thinking about problems is one of the main causes of a busy mind. Before you know it, you can end up stuck in a never-ending vicious cycle of stress-inducing problem-based thinking that lowers your levels of wellbeing. Until you learn how to stop thinking so much it's hard to even comprehend the vast amount of energy that is used up and the high level of preventable stress that is caused by the habit of unconscious thinking. It is my hope that you will discover the delights of thinking less, not only for your health but also your happiness and life success. I've found mind calm to improve every aspect of my life and I don't know anyone who hasn't ended up better off by reducing his or her engagement in the thinking mind.

You cannot fix a problem when the very
thing you are using to fix it is causing
the problem in the first place!

Thinking your way out of a problem that your mind has created doesn't work. Yes, you may come up with the occasional solution that appears to improve things. However, you won't have resolved the real root-cause of your problems, namely the unseen habit of judgmental thinking. So before you know it, your mind will think up a new problem to deal with and you will feel compelled to think your way out of yet another hole that the very mind you're using invented out of thin air.

LIVING WITHOUT THINKING

You can live very well without thinking so much. Does this sound like an unrealistic or unwanted suggestion? Do you enjoy thinking? Aren't there some problems that really do need thinking about? Perhaps you have a physical condition, or you're not sure how you're going to pay the bills or you have a relationship disagreement. In situations like these I'd definitely recommend doing something about it, but, not by thinking your way out of the problem, as there is a high chance it was overthinking that got you into the difficulty in the first place.

Cultivating mind calm by thinking less doesn't make you passive or mean you can't be proactive about bringing about a better set of circumstances. With mind calm, you will just go about it differently. Instead of thinking at length about your problems and potential solutions, you let go of thinking and make it a priority in these moments to be consciously aware. Doing so will allow quite magical things to happen. From the silence of your consciousness you will be better able to access your intuition and hear your wisdom. You will find the best way forward comes into your awareness without much thinking at all. You will simply know what is the best and right thing to do. By letting go of thinking about things as problems and with less focus on what you don't want, you will become more aware of new and unexpected inspirations and solutions. By allowing a little time to pass, you give problems the space they need to sort 'themselves' out – often without any fear or interference on your part.

From a more restful and Self-aware state of being, the right opportunity will often show up to help you make some money. Or the next time you speak to your friend the right thing to say brings a new connection where there was once conflict. Calming the mind brings forth a new way of living. With very little effort, trying, controlling or strategizing, you operate from a consciously creative headspace and live more from your heart.

HEALING WITHOUT THINKING

Within the context of self-healing, a calm mind is an absolute must. To give your body the rest it needs, you must be willing to release your grasp of the meandering mind. The more you think, the more your body experiences whatever you are thinking about. The body doesn't know the difference between what's real and imagined, so the body responds in very similar ways to whatever you imagine – as though it is happening in reality. Consider this: *How much of your day do you spend thinking about things that aren't happening right now?* The body is designed to handle temporary bouts of stress, but always thinking about stressful things is a very different story.

In my opinion, it is less the life events that negatively impact health, but rather the incessant thinking about them before and afterwards – with some people even caught in concerned thinking about things that never even happen. Constant thinking keeps you locked in a perpetual state of stress-inducing tension that disrupts the energetic equilibrium and balance of your body. In short, the more you think, the more you create an inner climate of *dis*-ease. The good news is the more you tame the thinking mind, the greater opportunity the body has to rest, recover and heal.

Stop the ineffective strategy

Thinking may appear to have helped you survive this long and along the way have brought you some satisfaction and success. But with mind calm you can experience a marvellous, multi-faceted fulfilment that allows supreme health to be savoured and enjoyed. I believe mind calm is the difference between an average and amazing life. The best news of all is that it can be your choice. It's within your reach and comes from letting go.

> *Creating mind calm is quicker and*
> *easier than you may think!*

To help you make the move from stress to serenity I'm excited to now teach you the first step of the Body Calm meditation technique. Affectionately called 'GAAWO', meaning 'Gently Alert Awareness Wide Open', it is a remarkably easy way to still your busy mind that quite literally takes less than a second to start benefiting from.

GAAWO

GAAWO is supremely simple. However, the mind can interfere in its proceedings, so I recommend that you do your best to adhere to the following three golden rules, not just the first time, but every time you use GAAWO:

Rule 1: Play with GAAWO

When you were a child you would play. While doing so, you would be curious, explore and not give up at the first hurdle. In fact, the hurdles were all part of the fun because you learnt how to jump even higher. Becoming adults we can forget how to play, often getting caught in the trap of trying to get it right first time. We can lose interest or give up, if we aren't immediately perfect at it and we can even talk ourselves out of it before we begin! To get the best from GAAWO you need to be willing to play. Give it a go, see what happens, jump higher than any judgement about it not working and keep GAAWO-ing until you get it. I assure you it's worth it and so would hundreds of people I've personally taught GAAWO to, who have loved it and enjoy the everyday benefits, too.

Rule 2: Don't think about GAAWO

You cannot think yourself into GAAWO. If you are thinking about GAAWO then you're going to be in your mind and you will end up one step removed from the experience of GAAWO. Without the experience, you will quickly come to the conclusion the technique doesn't work. It does. So stay aware of the difference between thinking about GAAWO and actually engaging GAAWO.

Rule 3: You can never do GAAWO later

All of your thoughts are about the past and the future, even thoughts about now. The moment is moving on before the commentator in your mind can start thinking about what's happening. So a common trick of the mind is the subtle planning to do GAAWO later. If you're not careful, you can find yourself thinking about how you really should do GAAWO, or that you will do it after the conversation, once you've sorted your problem or got home and are going to meditate. You can do GAAWO anytime and anywhere and if you don't, there's a high chance you are postponing it or planning to benefit from it later. Why wait, when you can be calm now?

Quite simply, if GAAWO appears not to be working for you, you can be sure that you are either forcing it instead of playing with it, or thinking about doing GAAWO or planning to do it later. But if you can play by the golden rules, you will gain great benefits from GAAWO. Happy with the rules? Let's get GAAWO-ing!

QUICK-START CURE: ENGAGING GAAWO

Looking at this page, as you continue to read the words in front of you, relax your gaze and let your field of vision spread out to the left and right. Do not look directly at anything to your left and right. Instead, use your peripheral vision to simply notice what is there. You may not be able to see it all clearly or in sharp focus, so it might be blurred. That's OK. Your intention right now is to gently, and without any forcing or straining, let your awareness open up wide to the left and right as you continue to look ahead at the words on the page.

Now, as you look at the words, notice what it's like to let your gaze open up wide, both upwards and downwards. In your peripheral vision you might be able to see your lap and the colour of the clothes you are wearing. Above you might see the ground beyond the book and/or the wall as it extends upwards to meet the ceiling (if you're inside somewhere). Irrespective of where you are or what you can see, just gently let your awareness open up wide to notice both above and below the page, simultaneously.

Continuing to look ahead at this page, now notice what it is like to let your gaze open up wide to the left and right, and above and below. What is it like to be gently alert with your awareness wide open? What's happening in your mind? Is it chaotically busy or more calm and quiet? Has your inner experience of this moment become more restful? Are you thinking about the past or the future, or are you present in the here and now? Can you notice an inner spaciousness or even stillness, as you engage GAAWO now?

When you engage GAAWO, you disengage the mind.

Remember the three golden rules. Play with engaging GAAWO without thinking about it or planning to do it later. Without stopping to think about it, what is it like to be gently alert with your awareness wide open, right now?

TOP TIP: DON'T FORGET TO BREATHE!

Breathing brings oxygen into and around the body, and oxygenated cells are healthier cells. When teaching GAAWO I often see people holding their breath. There's no need to do this! You need to breathe normally. So as you continue to engage GAAWO, you may want to relax your diaphragm and allow your belly to move in and out.

Due to the mind–body connection, you may notice that now you've brought more stillness to your mind, your body feels more relaxed. Allow this state to remain. You will also find that if at any point you start thinking again or become tense, you will have stopped engaging GAAWO. Be aware of this subtle disengagement of the technique because if you're not careful you can quickly start thinking GAAWO is ineffective. It's not. Time after time it's worked wonders for all who engage it as taught.

USE THE SELF-HEALING STATEMENTS

Throughout this book you'll find 'self-healing statements' that summarize the key shifts in awareness that I'm encouraging you to embody and know deeply. You may want to choose the ones that resonate strongly with you and simply read them often as quick reminders of the ideal attitude to adopt for healing and staying healthy.

SUMMARY: STOP STRESSING, START RESTING

- Body calm begins with mind calm.

- Most people spend most of their day thinking.

- The body feels and experiences mental movement.

- Excessive thinking causes your body stress.

- Constant thinking gives the body little time to rest.

- Thinking also creates problems because the mind judges everything when trying to make sense of it.

- You cannot solve a problem with the very thing that's causing the problem in the first place.

- Mind calm offers a healthier way of being and living.

- GAAWO = Gently Alert Awareness Wide Open.

- When you engage GAAWO you disengage the mind.

- Being aware, you experience the calm of consciousness.

- GAAWO is the first step to Body Calm meditation.

- To help the body heal, you must prioritize mind calm.

SELF-HEALING STATEMENTS: STOP STRESSING, START RESTING

I am much more than my mind.

I am the awareness that is aware of my mind.

I am the calm consciousness that is aware of now.

I am the awareness that is always well.

I am willing to let go of thinking so much.

I am open to seeing my mind not being my mind.

I am helping my body heal by calming my mind.

Chapter 4

THE BODY CALM
MEDITATION TECHNIQUE

The purpose of meditation is to rest within your real Self: the calm consciousness that is always within you. Through being conscious of your own consciousness, you can discover the aspect of your Self that never gets stressed, sick or suffers. Even if your body is uncomfortable or presenting undesirable symptoms, you can be well. By meditating, you stop letting your head get in the way of you being your Self, allowing you to more easily experience a radiantly rich life.

Being your real Self is the best medicine for your body.

More specifically, Body Calm meditation helps you to befriend your body, give it the rest it needs to recover and improve the communications happening within your mind and body. With regular practice, the meditation technique can help you to form new and improved beliefs, ones that encourage physical health, for life.

THE EASIEST THING YOU WILL EVER DO

Although these kinds of results may sound hard to achieve, in reality, accomplishing them needs to be one of the easiest things you ever do. Trying too hard, thinking too much, fighting your feelings and living in a limited way because of unhealthy beliefs saps your vital healing energy, while also putting strain upon your body due to the never-ending effort involved. I believe the stress caused by such a way of living is the very reason why we end up with physical problems in the first place. As a result, learning how to use less energy and rest more deeply requires a very simple way to meditate such as Body Calm.

We are conditioned to believe we need to work hard to be deserving of what we want to achieve. But Body Calm requires the exact opposite attitude.

Learning how to 'just be' requires a willingness to do less and *be* more. In this chapter you'll learn the three-step Body Calm meditation technique, which I'm confident you are going to love. Before you do, however, I want to make it explicitly clear that you must engage the 'steps' in the most unforced and gentle way possible. Trying, straining and controlling in any way during the process is counterproductive to reaching the state of stress-free harmony. You will find that the gentler you can be, the more quickly your mind slows down, allowing for deep rest.

With Body Calm you are removing the barriers to the body's inbuilt ability to heal and be healthy.

Consider this: the last time you got a paper cut, how much effort did you need to engage in to fix it? Very little, actually! The body knew how to heal and as long as you didn't do anything to prevent its work, it quietly and efficiently did its magic. Before you knew it, the cut had healed. Similarly, trust your body to do its silent work. Focus less upon trying to heal and instead aim to master how to be in the best state of relaxation.

Stress, emotional unease and unhealthy beliefs breed imbalance in the body, making it more likely to become ill. We will explore this more in Part II. So to get your Body Calm journey off to the best start, be willing to play with this meditation technique with the least amount of effort you can muster. Lastly, let me remind you that you are so much more than any temporary thoughts, feelings and body stuff. You are the permanent conscious awareness. It requires no effort to *be your Self*. With this in mind, the Body Calm 'steps' are not something you need to perfect and do 'right', but instead should be used to dissolve the habit of not being your natural Self. Although I will offer instructions, you have permission to not try to do the meditation right!

Trying to be good at Body Calm meditation is an unnecessary added pressure you don't need right now. By letting go of perfecting it, you'll get the results that are perfect for you.

CONSCIOUS AWARENESS LIFE MEDITATION

The 'CALM' part of Body Calm is an acronym that stands for 'Conscious Awareness Life Meditation'. Body Calm is therefore a way to meditate that cultivates the habit of being consciously aware in life. It is my hope that by now you have a heightened understanding and appreciation of why you want to be consciously aware and are feeling motivated to get meditating.

Body Calm involves two main elements:

1. Being Gently Alert with your Awareness Wide Open (GAAWO).

2. Occasionally thinking Body Calm Thoughts that help to heal the sources of stress.

Body Calm meditation can be used both with your eyes open and closed. In Chapter 3, I introduced you to GAAWO (*see page 35*), when you learnt how to be gently alert with your awareness wide open with your eyes open. Now it's time to play with GAAWO with your eyes closed. Whenever I first teach closed-eye GAAWO to people at my private clinic or public events, I notice they often jump to the conclusion that it's going to be harder. However, it need not be. Yes, you won't be able to see anything. But if you give it a go, you may be surprised by how natural it is.

ENGAGING CLOSED-EYE GAAWO

To make it super easy, ignore the 'wide open' part of the technique. With practice, you will notice it automatically happens the more you use it. Right now, as you are looking ahead at this page, I want you to first notice how effortless it is to gaze forwards and be aware of the words. It really takes zero effort. So as you gaze forwards at the page, I want you to let your eyelids drop down while maintaining your gaze forward. There's no need to tense your forehead or eyes; keep your muscles soft and relaxed. Continue with your eyes closed while being gently alert with your gaze forwards. You may find that your mind has become more quiet and still and there are fewer thoughts happening already. Now notice if you're accidentally holding your breath or tensing your diaphragm and let them release and become freer. Maintain a naturally balanced breathing pattern as you continue with your eyes closed and with your gaze forward for up to 20 seconds.

How did you get on? Was it easy, relaxing, silent and calming? Did you find your mind and body enjoyed a moment of restfulness?

Great! Now, if you feel ready, try it again, but with a wider gaze. Look ahead at the page and be gently alert with your awareness wide open. Allow your eyelids to drop down and close while continuing to gaze forwards and wide. Sit for up to 20 seconds engaging closed-eye GAAWO.

What happened? Nothing? Great!

If you were hanging out with GAAWO engaged you would have found very little happened in your mind. There may have been a couple of thoughts but there was also quiet calm present within you, which may even have felt still and spacious. If that was the case you can be sure that you were experiencing your real Self. Remember, consciousness is a peaceful, open, unmoving, presence. I encourage you to make it a priority to notice when you are calm and quiet and hang out there as much as possible when playing with Body Calm. (If you found the full GAAWO technique challenging, then play longer with the streamlined version of GAAWO, with only a forward gaze. With practice, your gaze will become wider and more open.)

GAAWO: The start of every calm sitting

Each Calm Sitting – which is the term for the more classic closed-eye sitting meditation – starts with closing your eyes and engaging GAAWO. Always stay in GAAWO for a while. I'm intentionally not telling you how long for so that you don't time it. Just be in GAAWO until it feels right to think a Calm Thought.

THE BODY CALM THOUGHTS

Calm Thoughts are short statements that you think occasionally during open and closed-eye Body Calm meditation. They give your mind something useful to do when it inevitably wants to become active after having engaged GAAWO for a while. They also serve to heal your belief system from the most common unhealthy beliefs that cause stress. Due to the fact that your mind wants to believe something, we are going to give it a series of healthy beliefs to adopt. These beliefs act as the antidote to any attitude that might have been having a detrimental effect upon your body, behaviours and life. The belief–body connection makes bringing these Calm Thoughts into your awareness a priority because they will improve the messages happening within the mind and body. As a natural consequence, your body will adapt and respond to reflect the presence of these positive messages. You will also find that because of your new belief system, you will naturally think, feel and behave in a more peaceful, positive and proactive way, with the end result being more harmony. Sound good? So what is a Calm Thought? A Calm Thought consists of three components:

I AM + POSITIVE VIRTUES + FOCUS POINTS

Component 1: I AM

Despite being two of the shortest words in the English dictionary, 'I' and 'AM' together are two of the most powerful ever to be thought or spoken. When you think or say 'I AM', you are referring to the absolute aspect of your Self that is unconditioned consciousness, unbounded being and infinite awareness. The phrase 'I AM' can be found in many religious and spiritual texts to describe the Supreme Being, with some groups and theologians believing 'I AM' to be the actual name of God. 'I AM' is a term that's been used over thousands of years to describe the divine nature of who and what we truly are. 'I AM' is the 'Stateless State of Supreme Reality', also known as 'Parabrahman'. 'I AM' is the underlying eternally pure awareness that is untarnished by mind-based perceptions. 'I AM' is therefore unrestricted by any labels, concepts, beliefs or self-imposed limitations. It is pure, powerful and infinite.

'I AM' is by far the most accurate way of describing your Self. It is the consciousness that we've spoken a lot about so far in this book and the still silent spaciousness that you can experience directly when using GAAWO. Putting your attention on 'I AM', by simply thinking the words, especially with GAAWO engaged, is therefore exceptionally powerful. It helps you to recognize and become aligned with the truth of Who You Are that exists beyond your beliefs and ideas around the identity that you think you are (I will speak more about this in Chapters 8 and 13.)

You are so much more than you think, and 'I AM' is a key to accessing the rich treasures of your real Self.

Within the context of Body Calm meditation, we use 'I AM' to remember and reconnect with the perfect, whole and complete consciousness that is beyond temporary mental, emotional, physical and life conditions. As it is a statement of truth and your beliefs are only ever relatively true, repeatedly thinking it can also dissolve any unhealthy beliefs you may have formed that may be harmful to your physical form and have been standing in the way of you getting the best from your body.

Component 2: Positive Virtues

To harness the power of 'I AM' to heal and stay healthy, we marry 'I AM' with a series of positive virtues. These encourage the mind to form healthier beliefs and help you to embody healthier states of being that support the body.

Whatever you attach to 'I AM' you become.

Over the years I've had the opportunity to observe a number of common beliefs held by people struggling with a range of physical health complaints, with 'I'm unsupported', 'I'm not good enough', 'I'm unworthy' and 'I'm weak' being a few of the most harmful. You become what you focus on the most, so, to help heal them, Body Calm meditation offers the opportunity to embody a series of positive virtues, which when thought and felt regularly enough can transform your belief system (*see page 50* for the complete list of Body Calm Thoughts). Due to the power of the mind–body connection, as you adopt a healthier attitude, your physical form can quickly adapt to give you a physical body that reflects the healthier mind-set.

TOP TIP: BE WILLING TO BE BOTH BELIEFS

In Chapter 8, we'll explore beliefs in much more detail and you'll discover that trying to create new beliefs while still in conflict with your former 'negative' ones can be both harder and more stressful. If any of the Calm Thoughts feel uncomfortable, it usually means there is a conflict with a currently held belief. Use the quick-start cure on page 111 on any Calm Thoughts that you find challenging. By being willing to be both – positive and negative – you collapse any conflict and allow the new attitudes to be more easily embodied.

Component 3: Focus Points

Each Calm Thought also has a recommended location within or around your body on which to put your focus when thinking it. With the inclusion of these focus points, the power of the Calm Thoughts is magnified significantly. Focus points work in a number of ways. First, a few of the locations sit within some of the well-known energy centres in your body called 'chakras'. Known and taught in many traditions, chakra is a Sanskrit word that translates as 'vortex'. By placing your attention on these areas of your body while thinking the Calm Thoughts, you not only activate the energy vortexes more but also harness their power to embody the positive virtues.

Not all of the focus points link with chakras. They don't need to. All are symbolic and appeal to the mind–body connection to help healing. For example, when it comes to the interconnectedness between the mind and body, most people I meet who feel they are 'unsupported' also tend to present lower back problems. So thinking 'I AM SUPPORTED' while focusing on the 'Base of the Spine' – which is in fact one of the Body Calm Thoughts – can heal the belief and perception that you are unsupported. By working in harmony with the symbolic nature of the mind–body connection, you reduce mental and physical resistance and more easily shape a new belief system.

Before taking you through the Body Calm meditation technique in detail, here's a quick reminder, so you can see how simple and easy this form of meditation is.

BODY CALM MEDITATION TECHNIQUE AT A GLANCE

Step 1: Engage GAAWO
Be Gently Alert with your Awareness Wide Open.

Step 2: Think Calm Thought
Think one of the Body Calm Thoughts (see page 50).

Step 3: Re-engage GAAWO
Be Gently Alert with your Awareness Wide Open.

When you notice tension in your body or that you've been thinking, repeat steps 1–3.

Always begin using Body Calm by engaging GAAWO. Then, once you are gently alert with your awareness wide open, think one of the Calm Thoughts. After you have thought the Calm Thought, let go of the words and the focus point by re-engaging GAAWO. Rest for a while doing nothing except being consciously aware until you notice tension within the body or that you've been thinking about something, then repeat the three steps. Easy! But believe me, it is the simplicity of Body Calm that makes it so profound and powerful in its healing benefits.

The 10 Calm Thoughts

There are a total of 10 Body Calm Thoughts, each consisting of 'I AM', a positive virtue and a focus point:

I Am + Virtues	Focus points
I Am Healed	In the Entire Body
I Am Enough	Far and Wide
I Am Worthy	Top of the Head
I Am Free	Forehead Centre
I Am Kind	In the Throat
I Am Open	In the Heart
I Am Calm	In the Solar Plexus
I Am Strong	In the Navel
I Am Supported	Base of the Spine
I Am Secure	Soles of the Feet

BODY CALM MEDITATION USING ALL 10 CALM THOUGHTS

Now you know the three steps involved in Body Calm meditation (*see page 49*) and the 10 Calm Thoughts, let's go through a complete sitting together.

- Begin by sitting comfortably, close your eyes, and engage GAAWO by being gently alert with your awareness wide open.

- Think I AM SECURE, with your attention on the soles of your feet... Let go of the words and the focus point by re-engaging GAAWO. Rest consciously aware until you notice tension or thinking.

- Then engage GAAWO for a short while before thinking I AM SUPPORTED, with your attention at the base of your spine... Let go of the words and the focus point by re-engaging GAAWO. Rest consciously aware until you notice tension or thinking.

- Now engage GAAWO for a short while before thinking I AM STRONG with your attention in the navel... Let go of the words and focus point by re-engaging GAAWO. Rest consciously aware until you notice tension or thinking.

- Engage GAAWO for a short while before thinking I AM CALM with your attention in your solar plexus... Let go of the words and the focus point by re-engaging GAAWO. Rest consciously aware until you notice tension or thinking.

- Next engage GAAWO for a short while before thinking I AM OPEN with your attention in your heart... Let go of the words and focus point by re-engaging GAAWO. Rest consciously aware until you notice tension or thinking.

- Now engage GAAWO for a short while before thinking I AM KIND with your attention in your throat... Let go of the words and the focus point by re-engaging GAAWO. Rest consciously aware until you notice tension or thinking.

- Engage GAAWO for a short while before thinking I AM FREE with your attention in your forehead centre... Let go of the words and the focus point by re-engaging GAAWO. Rest consciously aware until you notice tension or thinking.

- Next engage GAAWO for a short while before thinking I AM WORTHY with your attention on the top of your head... Let go of the words and the focus point by re-engaging GAAWO. Rest consciously aware until you notice tension or thinking.

- Engage GAAWO for a short while before thinking I AM ENOUGH with your attention far and wide... Let go of the words and the focus point by re-engaging GAAWO. Rest consciously aware until you notice tension or thinking.

- Now engage GAAWO for a short while before thinking I AM HEALED with your attention in your entire body... Let go of the words and the focus point by re-engaging GAAWO. Rest consciously aware until you notice tension or thinking.

- Either repeat the Calm Thoughts series (1–10) or if you're ready to finish the Calm Sitting, repeat 'I AM HEALED' three times before slowly opening your eyes.

ADDITIONAL OPTIONS FOR A CALM SITTING

Body Calm meditation offers a range of ways that you can use to suit your preferences and ever-changing needs. When it comes to sitting positions, always be physically comfortable. During sitting meditations, you may want to rest the palms of your hands in an upward-facing direction because it is known to be linked with receiving. Also, although we have gone through a complete Body Calm Sitting, in which you use all 10 Calm Thoughts once in the order they've been listed on pages 51–2, you are free to use them in whatever way works best for you. The most common four Calm Sitting options are listed below.

1. Use every Calm Thought

Follow similar instructions to the ones outlined above. Set the intention at the beginning of your Calm Sitting to use all 10 of your Body Calm Thoughts. Then close your eyes, engage GAAWO and go! You might think each Calm Thought only once before moving on to the next, which is good if you don't have much time. Alternatively, if you want to play longer, are feeling super stressed or want to make a concerted effort to heal a physical condition, you might use each Calm Thought a few times before moving on to the next.

2. Use only one Calm Thought

Start by considering what you would like to focus on most during the Body Calm Sitting. Perhaps you are aware that you have an unhealthy belief or a stressful habit you want to resolve. Or you may want to focus on healing a specific condition. Decide in advance upon the most appropriate Calm Thought to use. Once decided, close your eyes, engage GAAWO and get going with your focused Calm Sitting using only one Calm Thought.

3. Use the Calm Thoughts you tend to avoid

Begin by considering which of the Calm Thoughts you tend to feel uncomfortable using, or avoid altogether. Any avoidance or discomfort when using specific Calm Thoughts can mean there is a block or resistance that you could benefit from healing your relationship with. By giving them your time, attention and love you will find that any blocks to using the Calm Thoughts fade away and you may also notice improvements in the corresponding area of your body and life.

4. Use 'I AM HEALED' between each Calm Thought

Although it can take more time to do, thinking 'I AM HEALED' between each of the Calm Thoughts can be very powerful. Doing so repeatedly sends the very powerful message of already being healed to your body.

Calm Moments: Open-eyed practice

Remain in a restful state through your day by using Body Calm meditation with your eyes open through what I like to call 'Calm Moments'. For such moments, choose one of the Calm Thoughts you want to use during your day. Then, whenever you remember to do so, engage eyes-open GAAWO, think your Calm Thought and move on with whatever you were doing until the next time you remember and do it again. Calm Moments are especially useful anytime your attention moves to thinking about or focusing on your physical condition. By having open-eyed Calm Moments often, the results are magnified exponentially.

Recommended daily practice

Getting stressed, thinking too much and missing the present moment are unhealthy habits. For the best results, I recommend you do two or three Body Calm sittings every day, each lasting between 15 and 20 minutes to stay fit and healthy, and between

30 and 60 minutes (or more!) if you are suffering from a serious condition and are able to give your body as much rest as possible. Good times of the day are when you first wake up in the morning, mid-afternoon, before your evening meal or as you go to sleep at night.

Little and often is the best way to stay healthy; longer and more often if you need to heal!

THE PURPOSE OF EACH CALM THOUGHT

I've tracked the most common mind-based causes of physical conditions and have described these in Part III. The Body Calm meditation technique has been designed to directly support the healing of these potential causes. Simply meditating every day with Body Calm, you can help to heal the beliefs, emotions and life experiences that tend eventually to turn into physical conditions. To encourage you to use them, here's the purpose of each of the 10 Body Calm Thoughts:

1. I AM SECURE (soles of the feet)

Fear and insecurity activate the fight/flight/freeze response in the body. A concoction of stress hormones is released into the bloodstream and pumped around your circulatory system that reaches over 60,000 miles long. Although this is a natural process and can help you survive potential life-threatening situations, most events in life are far from being life-or-death encounters. Nevertheless, these stress hormones tell your body to remain in a state of high alert, which has been found to compromise health over time.

Thinking 'I AM SECURE' while focusing on the soles of the feet can help you to feel grounded and give your body permission to rest. It also allows you to relax into the Body Calm meditation, overall, helping to disengage the stress state, activate the relaxation response and maintain a calmer inner climate in which the body is more able to heal and remain healthy.

2. I AM SUPPORTED (base of the spine)

Feeling alone, isolated, separate and unsupported are very common feelings found in people presenting a range of physical issues. Believing yourself unsupported, or resisting supporting others, can cause physical issues to show up throughout the body, with the lower back being a common place for pain and other problems. Thinking 'I AM SUPPORTED' while focusing on the base of the spine can help to heal the perception that you are unsupported and allow you to see you are very capable of supporting yourself and others. It also enables you to see that you are much more supported than you may have realized.

3. I AM STRONG (in the navel)

Believing that you are weak or vulnerable are common causes of the body existing in a chronic state of fight/flight/freeze. Also, your mind will always find evidence to support your beliefs, so fear-based beliefs can cause you to filter reality in a way that makes the world appear scary. Inevitably, perceptions based in fear make us hide away from potential threats and never fulfil our purpose. Linked with vulnerability is often a heightened need for protection. This can lead to a number of physical problems, such as skin conditions and digestive disorders, and a depleted immune system – to name a few common issues. Thinking 'I AM STRONG' while focusing in the navel helps you to recognize your innate power and allow your body to have healthy levels of protection in place.

TOP TIP: POSITIVE POWER

'I AM STRONG' also creates a healthier relationship with the emotionally intense energies happening in your body. I believe that these emotions – often labelled as panic or anxiety – are your inner power rising up to help you to heal, create or change things in your body or life. It can be very powerful to let go of the labels 'panic' or 'anxiety' and instead refer to these energies as your 'inner strength'. Having had what I thought was anxiety for years, I discovered that I had been unintentionally suppressing my inner power because I believed the feelings were bad. However, if you are open to viewing sensations that you may have thought were panic as a positive power, you can use the energy in productive ways.

4. I AM CALM (in the solar plexus)

With an inner climate of calm there comes the harmony you need to rest and recover. Chronic anxiety and angst, on the other hand, along with a persistent sense of inner-uneasiness, tend to lead to *dis*-ease. Thinking 'I AM CALM' while focusing in the solar plexus not only cultivates calm, but also helps you to heal your relationship with your emotions. Befriending your feelings and learning how to be calm and comfortable, even when you have intense energy happening within the body, is a key part of Body Calm. Do not use this Calm Thought to get rid of uncomfortable emotions. Peace is not the absence of emotion, so use it with the intention of being in harmony with however you happen to feel. Doing so leads to less tension and more inner balance. (See Chapter 7 for more about healing your relationship with emotions.)

5. I AM OPEN (in the heart)

The heart and chest areas are linked with expansion and connection. Thinking 'I AM OPEN' while focusing in the heart helps you to open up the chest and heart area of the body, as you heal beliefs and experiences associated with feeling hurt, overwhelmed and disconnected. When a person goes through emotionally intense events, it is common for them to 'close' their heart area to avoid future hurt or discomfort. On the physical level, when the heart, blood vessels and arteries become closed or blocked, cardiovascular conditions become more likely. On an emotional level, however, the more open your heart, the greater your capacity to love and be loved.

6. I AM KIND (in the throat)

A healthy body is built upon a strong foundation of kindness, caring, compassion and forgiveness. The throat is linked with communication – both with yourself, other people and life. Thinking 'I AM KIND' while focusing in the throat helps you to cultivate compassionate communications and speak with gentleness. As your body feels and experiences what and how you speak, this can be very healing – not only for yourself, but the people who are touched by your words. Don't use this Calm Thought to hold back from saying what needs to be said: unsaid truths and unexpressed feelings can also lead to physical problems, especially pain. Instead, use this Calm Thought to cultivate the ability to communicate what you need to say and feel in the kindest way possible – so that you are gentle on your body and the other people in your life.

7. I AM FREE (in the forehead centre)

If you believe and feel that you are restricted, lack the freedom to choose your own destiny and are unable to be and do what you want, then your body can enter into a stressed physiological state due to the perception of being stuck, controlled and helpless. Also, if you get caught up in your mind in cyclical thinking patterns about perceived problems or potential threats then, again, your body tends to become tense. Thinking 'I AM FREE' while having your focus in the forehead centre often leads to complete mind calm, during which you have next to no thoughts whatsoever. When the mind is still, you are free from whatever you were thinking about and your body is able to rest more fully. Use this Calm Thought to regain the power to choose and let go of anything that's playing on your mind.

8. I AM WORTHY (top of the head)

Spiritual teachers over the centuries have said that 'you are what you seek', meaning that, if you want peace, love, joy, forgiveness, freedom, compassion, etc., you need look no further than your real Self. The reality is that when you become consciously aware, you rest in the aspect of your Self that is all these supreme states of being and more. However, one of the main reasons that you may not be experiencing these states is because you don't yet believe you are worthy. Overshadowed by the belief that you aren't worthy to have free access to these wonderful ways of being, you can end up living in the shadows of your real Self instead of within the light. Thinking 'I AM WORTHY' while focusing on the top of the head, you can open up to the inflow of positive virtues and give yourself permission to be present in beautiful states of being, now. This fulfils your purpose of living fully, while also creating the ideal inner environment for health to flourish.

9. I AM ENOUGH (far and wide)

Having discovered a whole host of beliefs that appear to restrict rest, hinder health and cause physical conditions, I've found that by far the most widespread and harmful beliefs are 'I'm not loved/loveable' and 'I'm not good enough'. It's no exaggeration to say these beliefs have shown up in at least 80 per cent of the people

I've worked with. Healing them is therefore vital. Despite your mind potentially having many reasons to justify the opposite, you are, in the reality of the present moment, loved, loveable and enough. The mind relies on reasons, judgement, comparisons and conditions, so if you are thinking instead of being aware, you are very likely to find evidence to prove your lack of love or 'enoughness'. However, when you let go of the mind and rest into your real Self, you find nothing is lacking or wrong with you. Consciousness is perfect, whole and complete, right now.

> *You can discover that love is what the presence of your being feels like.*

Thinking 'I AM ENOUGH' while focusing far and wide can help you to wake up to the reality that you are not confined to the boundaries of your body. You can recognize that you are fully deserving of love, without needing to do, prove or improve yourself in any way. By simply being here now, resting into the presence of your own awareness, your body can become a perfect reflection of your inner perfection.

10. I AM HEALED (in the entire body)

Your body is much younger than your chronological age. Research suggests that your stomach manufactures a new lining every three days, you grow a new skin every 28 days, while the cells of your lungs are regenerated every 2–3 weeks and your liver is renewed every 5 months. In fact, all aspects of your body are constantly regenerating with around 96 million new cells being born every second. Yes, that's every second!

> *With the birth of each new cell comes the potential for a new version of your body to be created.*

How the millions of new cells are expressed is largely down to the kind of environment they are born into and the quality of the communications within the mind and body. Quite simply, your body is listening and adapting to your every thought and emotion, so what are you communicating? Thinking about your illness and feeling bad about it can end up being a self-fulfilling prophecy. The more you focus on feeling sick or not being healed yet, the more your body is made to operate within a negative climate and keep re-creating the same old conditions.

The speed at which the body can heal, when given the right thoughts and emotions, has been shown with quite remarkable results. A few years ago, in Beijing, China, at a medicine-free hospital, a woman diagnosed with a cancer in her bladder measuring 4.5 cm (3 inches) in diameter was healed in under three minutes with the help of practitioners standing around her repeatedly chanting 'already healed'. Ultra-sound footage of the remarkable event showed the cancer dissolving to nothing during that short time. In a video about it, best-selling Hay House author Gregg Braden said the healing occurred 'within the presence of the language that heals' and that the key to the healing was the patient's belief in the process and the practitioner's ability to fully feel the experience that the patient was 'already healed'. This Calm Thought is an example of 'language that heals'. To magnify its power, while thinking it, let yourself feel it, too. Embodying the experience that 'I AM HEALED' while having your focus in the entire body can be very powerful indeed.

PLENTY TO PLAY WITH

The 10 Body Calm Thoughts are the foundations of the Body Calm meditation technique, however, there's more to play with. To aid your self-healing, you'll also find additional Calm Thoughts relevant to specific physical issues and conditions in the directories in Chapter 15. It is recommended that you use the 10 Calm Thoughts outlined here every day and then draw on the additional ones if you want to focus on any specific health problem(s). Do not use too many! Use no more than five extra ones that relate to specific conditions you are encountering.

Your body will respond better to depth and repeated use of a few Calm Thoughts rather than a shallow or scattered approach. You can include them in a complete Calm Sitting with the 10 other Calm Thoughts. Or, if you are doing more than one Calm Sitting per day, feel free to focus on the condition-specific Calm Thoughts during your other sittings. You can also use the additional Calm Thoughts within your Calm Moments. Whatever you choose to do, remember to always end every Calm Sitting by repeating 'I AM HEALED' three times before slowly opening your eyes.

MOTIVATION TO MEDITATE

Congratulations! You now know the Body Calm meditation technique and have been given a number of different ways to bring your Body Calm routine into your daily schedule. However, let's be real – meditation only works if you do it. You may already have a 'things to do list' that reaches a mile long and I'm recommending you add to it. So to inspire you to commit to a regular Body Calm routine, take a moment to remind yourself of why you want to use Body Calm. Do you want to heal a physical condition? Are you fed up with feeling frustrated, tired of feeling tired or sick of being sick? Are you craving more calm in your life? Do you want to perform to your potential on the track, yoga mat, in the office or in some other area of your life? Do you find it difficult to make decisions, struggle to sleep or want to bring healthier habits into your life?

Why do you want to use Body Calm meditation?

Reminding yourself regularly of your motivation to meditate can help you to sit down and close your eyes. It will also help you to keep calm and carry on with your practice when experiencing the most common meditation happenings that I'm going to share now.

SUMMARY: BODY CALM MEDITATION TECHNIQUE

- The purpose of meditation is to rest in your real Self: the aspect of you that is always well.

- You must engage in meditation in the most unforced and gentle way possible.

- CALM = Conscious Awareness Life Meditation.

- The Body Calm meditation technique includes three steps: Engage GAAWO, think a Calm Thought, re-engage GAAWO. Repeat the three steps whenever you notice tension in your body or that you've been thinking.

- Calm Sittings are the closed-eye practice and Calm Moments are done with your eyes open.

- For Calm Sittings, you can use every Calm Thought, use only one or use the Calm Thoughts you tend to avoid. You can also include I AM HEALED between each Calm Thought.

- The recommended daily practice is two or three Calm Sittings lasting between 15–20 minutes every day. You cannot over meditate, so use it more if you are actively healing something.

- Your body is constantly regenerating. How the new cells are expressed is largely down to the kind of environment they are born into and the quality of the communications within your mind and body.

- Remind yourself frequently of the big benefits of meditation and your personal motives, so your commitment to doing it regularly remains strong and steadfast.

The lotus leaf is often used to symbolize the 'infinite', and at first glance the BODY CALM logo looks like a person sitting in meditation. On deeper inspection, however, you can see that the up-reached arms also form an eye in the centre. It is therefore a symbolic representation and reminder of the purpose of Body Calm, which is to be consciously aware by being inwardly attentive to the Infinite I.

Chapter 5

WHEN THE BODY HEALS

A multitude of things will happen when you meditate. This is due to the natural by-product of the healing activity that takes place and the interplay between the mind and body. You must be aware of and accept these common meditation happenings, if you are going to get the best from Body Calm. In this chapter we clear up some of the many myths about what should and shouldn't happen when you meditate and explain why certain happenings are not only inevitable but essential and highly beneficial for self-healing and staying fit and healthy.

If you are unfamiliar with the healing side-effects of meditation, you will most likely become disheartened, frustrated and give up before your body benefits. It is tragic how many people miss out on the remarkable returns from meditating regularly because they've picked up a pack of lies about what should and shouldn't happen. Make sure you're not one of them!

20 COMMON BODY STRESSORS

Can you relate to any of the common body stressors?

WORK

1. High workloads
2. Tight deadlines
3. Difficult working conditions
4. Redundancy threats/realities
5. Unemployment and/or search for work
6. Business travel – daily commute, flights etc.
7. Long days at the office

LIFESTYLE

8. Lack of quality sleep
9. Bills, debt and money worries
10. Relationship tension and/or break-up(s)
11. Diet – processed foods, additives, dairy, etc.
12. Smoking, alcohol and recreational drug use
13. Strenuous exercise, sports and active hobbies
14. Moving house

ENVIRONMENTAL

15. Political climate
16. War on terror
17. Wi-Fi exposure
18. Pollution
19. Sudden or persistent noise
20. Extreme weather

WHEN THE BODY HEALS THE MIND MOVES

Over the years your body has gone through several stressful situations. Some of the stress will have been released during your weekends off, holidays, when you sleep and any other times you've had a chance to relax. However, with so much stress borne by your body, there's a big chance you will still have some residual stored stress that has stuck around. It is the natural tendency of your body to heal and it will do so whenever given the opportunity during times of rest. When you close your eyes, engage GAAWO and use your Body Calm Thoughts, your body relaxes and releases stress.

Meditation gives the body the long-awaited and well-deserved rest it needs to let go of stress and to heal.

Healing causes activity within your body. Stored stresses from the past hours, days, weeks, years or decades are finally released. Simultaneously, the body uses the calmer conditions to engage in whatever maintenance and repair projects require attention. All this means that when you meditate, stuff is going to happen in your mind and body that you want to allow rather than resist. To push away what happens is to prevent the body doing its healing work, and so the right relationship with the movement is required.

EIGHT COMMON MEDITATION HAPPENINGS

Here are the eight most common meditation happenings to expect and let occur, for your body to heal, stay fit and healthy and let meditation do its wonderful work:

Happening 1: Memories

Memories are one of the movements of the mind when meditating. These may include happy or sad, positive or negative, comfortable or uncomfortable ones. They may be memories from earlier that day or events that happened years ago. Irrespective of the subject matter or comfort level, you want to let all your memories come and go. Refrain from judging or analysing them. If they are positive, be careful not to lose your Self in reminiscent thinking. Or if they are memories you'd rather forget, do your best not to get drawn into the drama.

Why has this old memory come into my mind? Did I not deal with it during my recent therapy sessions? There is no benefit in thinking about it because doing so will slow healing. What you are witnessing during your Body Calm sitting is your body finally getting around to letting go. This is a very positive thing. Remember, you become attached to what you resist. Whenever you notice negative memories in your mind, simply engage GAAWO. Be heroic by rising higher than your mind-based judgements, resistances and attachments. Over time, you will find the memory fades away as you stop giving it your attention.

Happening 2: Dreams

Several stresses being released simultaneously can appear in your mind as abstract dream-like imaginings. Dreams are how your mind makes sense of a collection of stresses releasing at the same time, which explains why you tend to dream most when your body reaches its deepest levels of rest. When you notice you've been in a dream, don't fall into the mind trap of thinking about what it may be trying to teach you.

Dream interpretation encourages excessive thinking and distracts you from your present moment awareness. Although it can be fun and fascinating to try to discover the hidden meaning of dreams, if you want to heal then don't hold onto them. Continue with your Calm Sitting by engaging GAAWO to allow your body to keep going with its stress-releasing, self-healing activity.

Happening 3: Busy mind

Sometimes you will have a busy mind. When this occurs you want to rejoice rather than resist because your body is in the process of releasing a huge amount of stress and undertaking multiple healing and repair projects. During a busy meditation, it can be easy to start judging that it's a bad meditation or conclude it's not working. In moments like these you want to see the judgemental thoughts, without being the judge. To do this, stay vigilant of the voice in your head that sounds like you, as it will often suggest that you 'stop and try again later'. This voice is a thought, too, and if you let it dictate proceedings, you may well get up and walk away from an immensely healing meditation.

Lots of thoughts when meditating = lots of healing!

Mind Calm is not about having no thoughts. It's about keeping calm irrespective of the quantity of thoughts by being consciously aware. So if you have a particularly busy meditation, use it as an opportunity to practise 'peace with mind'. Watch the thoughts, knowing that you are the awareness that's aware of them. Remember, you are the sky and the thoughts are the birds. The sky doesn't care how many birds are flying through it or if they are positive or negative birds! If you ever have a problem with the quantity or quality of thoughts happening, then you are thinking *about* your thoughts. Be aware of this habit of the mind. Let thoughts come and go, while remembering they do so within the context of calm consciousness. More often than not, if you've had a busy meditation that didn't feel restful, you will be pleasantly surprised by how relaxed your body feels after you finish your Calm Sitting and by how clear your mind is for the following few hours.

Happening 4: Emotions

Thoughts fuel feelings, so when you have movement in your mind, you will inevitably feel emotions in your body. You want to play with being comfortable when feeling uncomfortable and experience what I like to call 'peace with emotions'. One way this is achieved is by noticing when you've fallen into *being* the emotions.

When you fall into feelings, you also engage in thinking about them, too. Emotions are never a problem until you start thinking about them. So, to find peace with your emotions, you need to find peace with the thoughts you are having about them. By *seeing* the mind, not *being* the mind, you will create some space to let the emotions serve their positive purposes. From a consciously aware perspective, you can calmly coexist with any energy that needs to happen. (See Chapter 7 for more on this.) Often when meditating your body will raise your energy levels while it's working on parts of your body that need more energy to heal. Trust your body's wisdom and let it have the energetic resources it needs to perform its work.

Happening 5: Body stuff

Physical sensations occur when stress moves around and out of the body. You might get an itch, a temporary twitch, or even have a passing pain show up somewhere in your body. Without remaining consciously aware with GAAWO, it is tempting to think about and judge it as bad or wrong. *What is it? Why is it here? How long might it stick around? How can I make it go away?* Although pain is obviously uncomfortable, if you start thinking about it too much, you will be more likely to start suffering as a result of the physical discomfort. This is because pain is a sensation but suffering is a mental and emotional experience that occurs when you think about it. Discovering this all-important distinction between pain and suffering can be the difference between battling with your body or calmly coexisting with it.

Some pain can be inevitable, but suffering is optional.

Pain is a symptom of blocked energy and incomplete events or experiences. At times, physical sensations will be a call to action that you want to listen to, act upon and explore. You may benefit from investigating and resolving the mind-based causes of the energy blockage (using the Embodying Exercise shared in Chapter 14). Or you might simply need to move around a bit, have a stretch or give the body area a rub to help release the energy. Saying that, there will also be times when you may benefit from not putting too much attention on it. Personally, when pain has presented itself, I've found the more present and still I become the less intense the sensations, sometimes with the pain disappearing completely the more present and aware I am. So play with it and experience the benefits of 'peace with pain' for yourself. Only you can know if you need to do something about it or if the best thing to do is nothing, except to be calm and to allow.

WHEN THE BODY RECALIBRATES

When you make a big, positive change or embody virtues that encompass higher states of consciousness, the body can need to recalibrate itself. When this happens the body can temporarily present physical symptoms such as colds, flu and viruses, or you may feel just tired or fidgety. These symptoms are both necessary and temporary. In fact, they've been happening your entire life, even if you haven't recognized them as such.

Growing into new states

Once I was in a relationship with a woman who had a young child. Every so often, as the child grew from a baby into a toddler, she would get sick with the occasional cold, virus or the flu, or just not be her usual happy self. What was fascinating to observe though was that whenever the symptoms started to recede, the little girl would be able to do things that she couldn't do prior to the symptoms. She could say words that were previously unpronounceable, was

able to hold her spoon properly, complete a jigsaw, balance
better on her feet and so on.

Although it can be more obvious in young children, this recalibration of the physical body – due to shifts in consciousness – continues throughout our life. In times like these, when symptoms present themselves, I believe the body is recalibrating itself to ground into the physical body the newly acquired states of consciousness.

You want to allow this to happen and be at peace with the physical symptoms if/when they occur. The recalibration is a natural and necessary mechanism that allows your body to house higher levels of awareness, which help you to be healthier and happier. For instance, within the context of the virtue of compassion, the degree of compassion you can embody is determined by the current calibration of your body. Therefore, it will recalibrate itself when your consciousness shifts to house the higher frequency state of compassion. The more you play with the Body Calm philosophy and techniques, the more deeply you will be able to embody the positive traits. Incidentally, just because you embody a virtue once, it doesn't mean life will never invite you to do so again. As you grow in awareness, your body will recalibrate to be able to house higher levels.

This recalibration is also sometimes confused with having a 'healing crisis' – the physical symptoms that occur after you've resolved an issue in your life. Personally, I don't like the term 'crisis' because even just saying it can put the body in a state of high alert. I prefer to drop the word 'crisis' and just view these physical symptoms as the body healing. Perhaps you've noticed flu symptoms come on soon after a very busy time at work finally finishes. Or perhaps a passing pain has appeared when you've made a big decision that had been on your mind for a while. At my clinic I've heard countless similar examples from clients, including knee pain after deciding to leave their job or an achy upper back after resolving an issue they'd been carrying.

*Your body has your back and is always
doing what it can to be healthy.*

Recalibration and healing symptoms like these usually pass speedily and are something to observe and not resist if they happen. Obviously, if you are ever concerned or if symptoms persist, contact your doctor. But don't forget to engage GAAWO and remain calm and conscious as you do!

Happening 6: Sleep and meeps

Sleep is one aspect of the mind–body relationship in which the body can override the mind. If the body needs rest, you will fall asleep when meditating. In fact, many people learn to meditate because they want to sleep better, with many reporting the symptoms of insomnia disappearing after using meditation for a while. Saying that, I don't recommend intentionally falling asleep every time. Doing so will reduce your time spent being consciously aware. So always have the intention to be gently alert when meditating. After all you are closing your eyes in order to wake up to your real Self.

In summary, you don't want to resist the natural needs of your body. If your body needs to sleep, it will and to resist this will only cause conflict and stress. At the same time, you also don't want to view your meditation sittings as an opportunity to have a nap. I refer to these sleepy meditations as 'meeps' – sleeps that start off with a short meditation! Remember: aim to remain gently alert.

TOP TIP: STAYING AWAKE WHEN CLOSING YOUR EYES

To remain awake when closing your eyes to meditate, make the following adjustments to your routine:

- While staying physically comfortable, sit upright keeping your head over your shoulders. You will find the further back your head rests, the less alert you will be.

- Shorten the length of time of your Calm Sitting. It is more useful to do 15–20 minutes than a sleepy meander through an hour.

- Take some exercise before you meditate to be more physiologically alert; it doesn't need to be too strenuous, but some form of movement is useful.

- Drink a glass of water before beginning and meditate before you eat. The fuller your stomach, the more likely you are to be groggy and fall asleep.

Happening 7: Calm and contentment

Now for some meditation happenings, which are probably much more in line with what you were hoping for! Using Body Calm to let go of your thinking mind and therefore judgement, resistance and attachment, you will feel peace, love, contentment and happiness. Even better, these enjoyable experiences will often happen for no obvious reason, spontaneously rising up from the realms of your inner being. In other words, they don't happen because of any positive thought or a pleasing set of circumstances. Instead, they are the by-products of *being your Self*.

Happening 8: Still, silent spaciousness

Consciousness is supremely still, silent and spacious. Consequently, as you become more Self-aware i.e. you become aware of the aspect of your Self that is aware, your inner experience will be still, silent and spacious. During your Calm Sittings, whenever you notice these traits being present, simply allow them. In these moments you are beyond the movement of your mind and resting in your real Self.

In the same ways that peace is not the absence of emotions, stillness is not the absence of movement and silence is not the absence of sound. Stillness and silence are the constant context of movement and noise (see Chapter 13 for more on this). Playing with being aware of the inner still, silent presence changes your relationship with the movements in the mind and life. You become more willing to let them come and go and are less affected by the content of your thoughts, emotions and physical sensations when they happen. This is very liberating and leads to a more harmonious and happy life.

BODY CALM MEDITATION MIND-SET

Possessing the right mind-set is paramount. By sharing the happenings when the body heals, it is my hope that you are willing and able to let them occur and go. As you've learnt, there will be times when you enjoy deep peace and perfection and times when it may be downright busy and bewildering! If you're only going to meditate when it's calm and comfortable, you're going to miss out on meditation's massive healing rewards.

Meditation mind-set 1: Childlike curiosity

If meditation ever becomes difficult, tense, boring or unpleasant you will be lacking a childlike innocence in these moments. With such curiosity, you are open and excited about whatever may happen. You aren't holding any preconceived ideas about how you should feel or the quality or quantity of thoughts that should happen. You are open to absolutely anything. There's no room for boredom because you are so curious about what might happen. With childlike innocence, you approach meditation with wide-eyed wonder and a willingness to allow all that happens.

There are no 'good' or 'bad' meditations, only some that meet your expectations and others that don't.

Without childlike curiosity, you can end up in conflict with what happens and cause meditation to become counterproductive to your self-healing. Take a moment to consider what you don't want to happen and what you think must happen for you to have a 'good' Calm Sitting. Are you attached to having an empty mind, feeling peaceful or the pain going away immediately? Are you resistant to falling asleep, remembering certain memories or feeling uncomfortable occasionally? Then, once you are aware of these things, rise above resistance and appease the attachments by keeping an open mind. You will find that by being willing to turn towards what you don't want with a 'bring it on' attitude, your resistances and attachments lose their power to negatively impact your meditation experience negatively.

Assume if it's happening, it needs to happen

If thoughts become busy, let them. If emotions are particularly intense, befriend them. If uncomfortable physical sensations pass through, observe the body doing its best, while it finally gets some well-deserved rest. As an added bonus, if you can possess an attitude of unconditional allowing when meditating, you'll find this mindset spreads out to benefit the rest of your life, too. When unexpected or unwanted circumstances occur, you default to 'bring it on', don't end up in conflict with life and enjoy better health and happiness as a result.

Meditation mind-set 2: Keep GAAWO-ing

Meditation works if you commit to a regular routine. Perhaps, paradoxically, it is simultaneously a quick fix while also being a long-term winning strategy. Engaging GAAWO creates immediate mind and body calm, but it can take time for physical changes to take place. As a result, to get the results you want, you must keep doing it!

In my observations, the people who get the most from meditation all have one thing in common: they commit to doing their closed-eye practice every day and their open-eyed Calm Moments whenever they remember. They practise, even if they don't always feel the immediate benefits or think they are too busy to fit it in. They find the time and stay focused on the end goal, while maintaining an eye on the present moment. They know that they have everything to gain by keeping calm and carrying on.

SUMMARY: WHEN THE BODY HEALS

- Due to the mind–body connection, a multitude of things will happen while you meditate.

- When the mind is still the body relaxes. When the body rests it heals.

- Over the years you may have picked up lots of stress that will need to be released when you meditate.

- There are eight common meditation happenings, including:
    - » Memories
    - » Dreams
    - » A busy mind
    - » Emotions
    - » Body stuff

> » Sleeps and meeps

> » Calm and contentment

> » Still, silent spaciousness

- When these happenings occur, you need to see the judgemental thoughts about them that go on in your mind. Observing the thoughts helps you to gain peace with whatever needs to occur.

- When you have a shift in awareness, your body often needs to recalibrate to house the higher levels of consciousness. Physical symptoms can sometimes present themselves at these times.

- To get the best from meditation you require a mind-set of childlike curiosity and to be willing to 'keep GAAWO-ing' at times when you can't be bothered, believe it's not working or don't have time.

Part II

HARMONY HEALS

Chapter 6

CAUSES OF CONDITIONS

Why is my body not working as it should? Not knowing can be incredibly confusing, concerning and frustrating. Although there tends to be a lot of research available on *what* your physical condition is, what it's called and what's not working properly, it's often harder to find information about why it's happening in the first place. By no fault of their own, doctors are experts in diagnosing conditions and prescribing the appropriate drugs or interventions to treat symptoms. However, they are rarely trained in, or equipped with, the ability to explain exactly why the body creates certain physical conditions.

TREATING SYMPTOMS OF SYMPTOMS

Medical professionals, taught by classical institutions, are often trained to view and treat the body as separate from the mind and the soul. From this inevitably limited perspective, physical problems can only ever be the result of physical causes. You're gaining weight because your thyroid isn't working properly. You're feeling ill because you have a bacterial infection. You've got pain in your joints because you have arthritis. Or you have irritable bowel syndrome because you have a food allergy. Although it is not necessarily obvious at first, upon deeper examination, these explanations aren't diagnosing the cause. At best, they are diagnosing a symptom of another symptom, with the real root-cause remaining unknown.

Since I was a young child, I've been fascinated with the question 'why'. This is perhaps why I've always focused on exploring the subtle underlying reasons for why things happen. Not satisfied until I've dug as deeply as I can possibly go, I have been on a decade of discovery through my clinical practice to discover what really causes the body to get sick, why some people do and others don't, and how you can make positive changes to bring the body back to better health.

Taking the above examples further, being told you're gaining weight because of your thyroid is not being told the cause. It merely begs the next question: *Why is my thyroid not functioning as it should?* Being told bacteria in the body is the cause of your sickness, again falls short. *Why is there a build up of bacteria? Why are the joints swelling in the case of arthritis and why has the body become allergic to certain food types? Is it wear and tear, because it 'just happens sometimes' or simply bad luck?* Again, answers like these don't satisfy the curiosity that comes from asking why.

UNDERSTANDING THE UNDERLYING CAUSES

In the 19th century, a French chemist called Louis Pasteur came up with the Germ Theory of Disease, which ended up shaping a massive part of the modern medicine mind-set. He suggested that it was the microorganisms that invaded humans and other living hosts that caused disease. In quick succession, a majority of the medical authorities accepted this proposition and it became a common explanation for why people got sick and has shaped the mass use of medicines such as antibiotics ever since. This is despite Louis Pasteur himself acknowledging before his own death that his theory was, in fact, wrong. In the end, Louis quite rightly, in my opinion, concluded that germs could not cause infection without an underlying reason that was already present.

Louis' late realization makes much more sense, especially when you take into account the fact that not everyone, when exposed to the same bacteria or viruses, for example, ends up getting sick. Saying that, I can also appreciate why his original theory was so popular, perpetuated by the point that where there is illness there is often also microorganisms such as bacteria present. However, to blame bacteria or viruses as the ultimate cause, simply because they both tend to be present where there is illness, is a misguided assumption. Doing so is the equivalent of blaming fires on firemen. Yes, where there are fires there tend to be firemen, however, it is clear that the presence of firemen doesn't mean they are causing the fires – quite the opposite! Similarly, just because bacteria, for example, are present in the body in close proximity to where there's illness, it doesn't mean they are the ultimate cause.

DOCTORS DO GREAT WORK

For the record, I have a great deal of respect for doctors and have turned to them myself when I've had the occasional accident, been in need of stitching up or sought understanding about what's happening within my body. But beyond that, I've learnt to rely more on other integrative means when it comes to explaining, exploring and resolving the ultimate causes of any physical issues. So much so that I've had the privilege of working with people from around the world to help them to find and fix the mind-based causes of their own physical conditions. Over the years I've been blown away by the impact the mind has within the body and how by once and for all resolving the mind-based reason(s) for illness, the body can quickly and elegantly heal itself.

Obviously, not all conditions can be linked to the presence of bacteria or viruses. These are just a couple mainstream examples that help to demonstrate the rather limited mind-set of modern medicine, which looks to find physical causes to explain what happens within the body. With Body Calm, you are encouraged to let go of the assumption that there's *must* be a physical cause for your physical condition, by exploring and resolving the possible mind-based reasons, too.

THE MIND-BODY MIRACLE

Being proactive in your own self-healing requires you to go beyond what you've been conditioned to believe about the causes of conditions. To do this, you need to gain an appreciation and understanding of the intimate interconnectedness between the mind and the body within the context of the soul and life, and then be open to making changes to support the body's return to radiant health.

Every facet of the body is responding to whatever your mind believes, perceives and experiences.

One of the pathways of communication between your mind and body is via your autonomic nervous system (ANS). Your ANS regulates your blood pressure, heart rate, digestion and metabolism, along with many more of the 'automatic' functions of the body. Everyday examples that reflect the mind–body connection include your face turning red when you are embarrassed or having butterflies in your stomach when you feel nervous.

Although we often take these everyday examples for granted, it pays dividends to observe and appreciate the mind–body connection in action. For your face to turn red, thousands of chemical reactions need to take place, along with blood redirection to your skin. Interestingly, your butterflies are the sensation caused by blood draining from your stomach lining as it is sent to the external areas of the body to help you resist or run from the perceived threat.

I recommend monitoring your mind–body during the day. Notice what happens in your body when you recall certain memories, think about someone you dislike or love, criticize or praise something or experience a range of situations, such as being stuck in traffic or watching the news. Monitoring the mind–body reactions is a big leap in your self-healing journey. By observing the mind–body connection first hand, you will quickly see how your thoughts *are* impacting your body – all of the time. Knowing this, it makes much more sense for you to want to heal the potential mind-based causes of conditions, which I'll share in this part of the book, and feel motivated to use the exercise and directories provided in Part III.

THE BY-PRODUCT OF A BLOCKED BODY

Imagine crystal clear spring water gently flowing down a mountainside stream. If you were to drink from it, you'd find the water cleansing, nourishing and life supporting. Now, consider what happens to the water if it becomes stuck, unable to flow and stagnant. Over time it becomes toxic. The same water, which was once pristine, cleansing and beneficial for the body, is now poisonous. I believe something similar happens within your physical form when you are stressed. The body is an energetic system that is designed to remain healthy as long as its energy flows free. However, when it becomes blocked or restricted, this can cause a host of physical reactions including an upsurge in toxicity that is harmful to health.

As toxicity levels increase, so does your susceptibility to illness. Toxicity creates an inner climate that is the perfect breeding ground for bacteria, viruses and other factors linked with the presence of physical conditions. At the cellular level, toxicity is highly destructive, leading to the decay and weakening of the cells and making them more prone to disease. Furthermore, when the body reaches its toxic limits, it gets stimulated into doing what it can to survive. The body protects itself by surrounding toxins with fat cells and then moving them away from the essential organs, mainly to the bottom, tummy, legs and the backs of the arms, so leading to weight gain.

Another way the body protects itself is by releasing the toxins through the mechanisms and passageways of elimination. It uses the detoxification organs, including the liver and the kidneys, to release the build-up through symptoms like colds, the flu and diarrhoea to name a few – although symptoms are not limited to these common issues, these examples are the most recognized. Other less obvious symptoms are inflammation, skin conditions, foggy-headedness and lethargy.

Counterproductively, when confronted with physical symptoms like these, which are often uncomfortable or inconvenient, we follow the social norm and reach for a potion or a pill to deal with the discomfort. This quick-fix mind-set of using medicines that often work by suppressing the symptoms restricts the body's attempts to detox.

Acidity also goes hand in hand with toxicity, which means the body loses its acid-alkaline balance and again creates an inner climate more inclined to illness. Conditions like cancer have been found to find it hard to exist within alkaline environments and many other illnesses can be linked back to toxicity and acidity and the body's release responses in an attempt to protect and recover.

Illness and disease struggle to sustain themselves in an alkaline and energy-abundant inner environment.

Many of the physical symptoms that people are dealing with today are, in my opinion, the body's response to energetic blockages – its valiant attempts to protect itself by releasing toxins and resolve acid-alkaline imbalances. Therefore, to heal the physical causes of health problems – which are often linked with blockages, toxicity and acidity – you need to explore what's preventing your body from performing its functions. Knowing these underlying causes of poor health, your self-healing strategy becomes simple: to be and do what you can to help your body to cultivate a more harmonious and energy-abundant inner climate.

STRESS AND THE SUPPRESSION OF SELF-HEALING

Although short stints of stress can have the effect of boosting immunity and raising levels of certain cancer-fighting molecules, being in an never-ending state of stress is a very different story. Stress causes the body to turn off building-and-repair projects, speeds up the aging process, reduces immunity and, again, creates the perfect inner climate for a host of health problems to prevail.

When you are stressed you become tense, which restricts the movement of energy within your system and negatively impacts the toxicity and acidity levels within the body. The brain orchestrates the release of a concoction of stress chemicals, which prevents the cells from functioning properly and compromises their ability to take in proteins and eliminate toxins. This means that during prolonged periods of stress, at a cellular level, your body becomes increasingly toxic and is slowly starved of the nutrients it needs to sustain life.

As the well-known phrase goes: 'as above, so below'.
Whatever happens within the cells determines
what happens within the body as a whole.

Stress is not the cause of conditions, though. Conflict is. Without the inner push-pull fight between resistance and attachment, there exists a naturally calm climate that encourages energy to flow freely. During my extensive clinical practice, I've observed a number of subtle sources of stress and disharmony that appear to result in *dis*-ease and physical conditions. Although there are obviously some purely physical factors, such as processed foods, lack of exercise and environmental pollutants, in my experience, the majority of conditions are mind-based.

Seven secret sources of stress and quick-start cures

The following seven secret sources of stress coming up in the next chapters are what I've observed to be the usual reasons people lose harmony within their mind, body and soul, leading to sickness. I hope that by sharing them with you, you will be empowered to play an active role in your own self-healing journey, by cultivating the harmonious inner climate your body needs for life-long health and vitality.

To get the most benefit from these secret sources, use it as an opportunity for some honest self-reflection. I'm not saying that you necessarily have to work through each and every one of the causes. Such a task could appear quite daunting, while some may not even be relevant to your life. However, I do strongly recommend reading all seven and if any resonate with you, take note and apply the recommended quick-start cures.

Lastly, before you begin, I invite you to take a moment to pause and reflect upon the great work you are doing here. I for one am in awe of your desire to take the destiny of your health into your own hands and embark on a journey towards a healthier and happier life.

*Embrace and enjoy your self-healing journey because
it is your personal path towards the attainment
of the life purpose for which you were born.*

Chapter 7

UNCOMFORTABLE EMOTIONS

Emotions are an intrinsic and inevitable part of being human. During your day-to-day life, you will experience a whole host of feelings, with some comfortable and others less so. When it comes to enjoying better health with Body Calm, you need to learn to be at peace with how you feel. Now, you may notice I didn't just suggest that you must 'get rid of your negative emotions'. This is because Body Calm goes beyond managing and controlling emotions to give you genuine emotional freedom, whereby you can be in harmony with however you happen to feel in any given moment.

Befriending your feelings gives you a liberated life.

Without learning how to be in harmony with your emotions you can find yourself engaged in a fight against your feelings, causing much unnecessary mental suffering and physiological stress. You need energy to remain alive and your body needs that energy to be flowing freely. However, if you resist and suppress certain emotions, then the energy that your body needs to function properly ends up blocked and prevented from fulfilling its many positive purposes. Helping your body to heal therefore involves healing your relationship *with* your emotions with the ultimate goal of mastering the ability to allow your feelings to flow, by learning how to be comfortable with occasionally feeling uncomfortable.

CONDITIONED TO CONTROL EMOTIONS

Growing up, it is rare to be taught to feel emotions fully. Many of us were brought up by adults who were unwilling to experience the whole range of their *own* emotions and we were usually told to tone down or turn away from the intense ones that were perceived as problematic. We were also taught that some emotions were positive and others negative and it is common to be conditioned to avoid the 'bad' ones at all cost. This has lead to many growing up fearing their feelings, trying to constantly control them and believing that it is somehow wrong to feel 'bad' sometimes.

My interest in mind, body, spirit came about because I wanted to feel positive. I could feel lonely in a room full of people. I secretly suffered from on-going underlying anxiety, which could take my breath away; and at times felt really quite low. I wanted to make all the bad feelings go away, for good, and only feel purely positive – which seemed a perfectly reasonable goal to me. However, through my coaching, therapy and meditation work, a new relationship with my emotions has emerged. Instead of trying to always feel what my mind thinks are the 'positive' ones, I've learnt how to be more at peace with however I happen to feel. In doing so, I've found that the energy in my body has become better able to flow, serve its purposes and support me in enjoying an amazing life.

Along the way, I've observed key shifts in my awareness, which if taken on board and applied, can bring about emotional freedom, fantastic health and life fulfilment. I invite you to explore them for yourself now and see how your body and life can transform for the better.

AWARENESS 1: I AM NOT MY EMOTIONS

In an earlier chapter I asked: *How do you know you have a mind?* The answer was: you know you have a mind because you are aware of it. I then went on to explain how conscious awareness is the permanently present part of you, with your temporary thoughts coming and going within it. The same question works really well for emotions, too. *How do you know you have emotions?* Again, you know you have emotions because you are aware of them. In the same way as thoughts, consciousness is aware of emotions. Furthermore, if you consider how many emotions you've had over the past couple days, you may be able to recall anything from five to 15 or more. The number really doesn't matter. What's important is that you've had more than one because this shows your emotions are temporary.

> *Despite emotions coming and going, there is an aspect of you that's been present the entire time.*

Temporary visitors transiting through

Although you have air in your lungs as you read this, you are not the air you breathe. Air is one of the many temporary visitors existing within your body only for short amounts of time. Similarly, you are not the food you eat, water you drink and so on. Your body uses these things to create new cells and they also play an important role in helping you to remain alive. But even though they happen within you, they are temporary and therefore not your real Self. Emotions are also visitors passing through your body. They exist within you for a finite period of time to serve particular purposes, before moving on to then be replaced by some other transitory emotion. Explore this for yourself by asking:

What emotion am I currently feeling?

91

Has there ever been a time in my life when this emotion was not present?

What has been present the entire time?

Knowing you are not your emotions naturally changes your relationship with them. If they are not you, then you can more easily let them come, hang out and go when they're ready to do so. You don't need to fight or fear any feeling because you are so much more than any transiting energy. You are the vast consciousness, within which emotions occur and similar to the big and beautiful blue sky with birds flying through. By being the sky through resting aware of the big calm of your consciousness, you don't take emotions so personally and can let them perform their purpose as they pass through.

AWARENESS 2: PEACE IS NOT THE ABSENCE OF EMOTIONS

Two years after I started meditating regularly I went to my meditation teacher to tell him that I didn't think it was working. Knowing that the meditation was in fact working and it was only my expectations that needed some help, he enquired: 'How do you know the meditation isn't working?' I explained that I was still feeling anxiety in my solar plexus area. His response was nothing short of mind-blowing. With a big smile he declared, 'Peace is not the absence of emotions.' At first, my mind couldn't even compute the statement! Peace is not the absence of emotion? How could I experience peace, if I was feeling anxious? It made no sense at all. However, through exploring it, these seven words became one of the biggest things I've learnt during my meditation journey.

Without realizing it, I'd picked up beliefs about what peace was. I had beliefs about what peace would feel like and what had to happen to experience it. Peace had always eluded me because I had assumed it was a state of no emotion. But because I was human and therefore experiencing emotions all the time, I felt I was failing somehow at being peaceful. However, since exploring the possibility that peace is not the absence of emotions, I've discovered that I don't need to make them go away before I can experience peace.

Having 'peace with emotions' enhances harmony.

Learning how to be at peace with how you feel is key and, within the context of Body Calm, is achieved by being aware of the consciousness that's observing your emotions. The more Self-aware you can be – i.e. aware of the aspect of yourself that is aware – the more you directly experience a peace that is permanently present and an unconditional calm that is perfect, whole and completely untouched by any temporary feeling. To make sure you understand the magnitude of this shift in awareness, allow me to set out what I'm saying more succinctly:

Consciousness is aware of your emotions

Consciousness is already and always peaceful

Therefore, peace is aware of your emotions.

Get it? Consciousness is aware of your emotions and your consciousness is calm. Stay with me and remain open minded! I appreciate that you might have invested a huge amount of time, effort and money in the search and acquisition of 'peace of mind'. And now I am suggesting that you don't need to wait a second more or spend a single penny extra because the peace you seek is aware of your mind, within you now, waiting to give you what you've always had. There is no need to wait for your negative emotions to go away before you can feel calm and enjoy emotional freedom. Once again:

Peace is aware of your emotions.

Conscious awareness is inherently calm, which means that peace-filled consciousness is the context of every single apparently unpeaceful emotion. Peace is not the absence of emotions as it is the context of every emotion. To discover this for yourself, engage GAAWO because it is one of the easiest ways to be your real Self and to experience the peace that is always present. With GAAWO engaged, you can feel your calm consciousness, even if 'negative' emotions continue to be present.

AWARENESS 3: THE MORE EMOTIONS THE BETTER

Energy, life force, 'get-up-and-go' or whatever you prefer to call it, is without exaggeration the difference between life and death. Without it you're a goner and with it you are highly likely going to be a go-getter. Consider this: *What can you do with no energy?* Not very much! Anyone who's ever experienced chronic fatigue symptoms or been totally worn out will know this all too well. The body needs as much energy as possible to properly perform its functions and help you perform yours. You need energy for creating radiant relationships, enjoying your hobbies and making a positive difference in the world. In short, if you want to be successful in life, you need energy, and lots of it!

Emotions are 'energy in motion'. They are one of the main channels that energy moves within your body. Suppressing your emotions is therefore one of the quickest ways to block your life force and limit your ability to create abundant health. Stuck energy that is stagnant not only has the potential of becoming toxic but, if not allowed to flow, then ends up prevented from fulfilling its healing functions. I first learnt about the benefits of 'feeling my feelings' when I discovered the philosophies of the Hawaiian Kahunas. Documented as being powerful healers and manifestors, the Kahunas had a simple yet profound approach to life: Do things that bring you energy and stop doing things that take your energy away.

Believing that 'mana' (their word for life force or energy) was the difference between life and death, and one of the most precious resources a person can have at their disposal, much of their work revolved around building up energy reserves. Living in accordance with their philosophy, they would never intentionally suppress their emotions. To do so would fly in the face of everything that they did to help them be such great healers. Instead they would relax the body and breathe deeply to allow their emotions to flow as much as possible. They would welcome emotions and harness their healing power.

It is no coincidence that when you have a physical condition you can often have more intense emotions, too. I believe this can be because the body raises its energy levels to help healing.

Feel your feelings without getting lost in them

Accelerating your ability to self-heal is a big beneficial by-product of feeling your feelings. But it comes with an all-important caveat. To feeling your feelings in a way that aids your return to energetic equilibrium and harmonious health, you need to do so while remaining Self-aware. I highlight this because when told to feel their feelings, people often get lost in them due to their lack of conscious awareness. Instead of observing the energy from a Self-aware state, they drop into identifying with the sensations. If the energy is uncomfortable or appears 'negative', all too often it can lead to turmoil, suffering and dwelling in the thinking mind again. Doing so is not only highly stressful upon the body, but also not very pleasant to say the least.

Feel your feelings to let the energy flow free.

Feeling feelings in a consciously aware way therefore requires you to engage GAAWO while breathing naturally. Through the engagement of GAAWO, you will remain the observer and not get lost in your thoughts about the emotion or in the feelings themselves. The breath tends to become restricted whenever a person doesn't want to feel fully; so breathing helps to maintain a physiology that makes it easier for the energy to move. As mentioned before, if you are consciously aware then you will be resting in the calm consciousness that's aware of the emotions. You will find there won't be any need to struggle or suffer, even if the energy is intense and potentially uncomfortable. As this is potentially a new way to relate to and 'be' with your emotions, if you ever do find yourself falling into the feelings, I recommend the following simple protocol.

QUICK-START CURE: PASSING THROUGH

Lost in your emotions? Struggling to engage GAAWO? Resisting how you are feeling? In moments like these, when you're falling into your feelings, do the following:

1. Ask: *What emotion am I aware of right now?*

2. Ask: *Where do I feel the emotion in my body?*

3. Once you've named and located the emotion, turn your attention towards it and say in your mind or aloud the following: *Hello energy, thank you for passing through. You are welcome to hang out as long as you want.*

This simple statement holds within it the intention to allow rather than resist, which reduces any stress or suffering as a result of the fleeting feeling.

Being comfortable feeling uncomfortable

Body Calm gives you a healthier relationship with how you feel. It's not about manipulating or getting rid of your emotions, but learning how to be comfortable with any emotional energy by being aware of your real Self. You will continue to feel the whole spectrum of energies. Sometimes you will feel happy or sad, angry or amenable, fearful or immensely free. Therefore to help your body to heal you need to learn how to be comfortable feeling uncomfortable, so that you don't suppress your essential healing energy.

Even if I teach people this, they will often report back later saying that they felt 'bad' and did some technique to try to feel better. In response, I will be glad that they had temporary relief, but will also remind them that they aren't necessarily exploring the big benefits possible from healing their relationship with their emotions. This is because if they keep using techniques to change how they feel, they will stay stuck in the cycle of emotional manipulation instead of waking up to true emotional freedom.

Emotional freedom
= Peace with all emotions.

Uncomfortable emotions are a common cause of bad health – not due to the emotions themselves, but the relationship that most people have with them. It is not the emotion that causes *dis*-ease, but the resistance towards the 'bad' ones and the attachment to the 'positive'. Fighting your feelings blocks the energy you need to heal and can lead to harmful stress-induced side effects such as toxicity, acidity and imbalances.

Suspend judgement to stop suffering

As I described earlier, one of the main reasons why we resist uncomfortable emotions is due to having been conditioned to judge them as negative: growing up you were most likely taught labels for the different energies that happen and in the process learnt which were positive and which were negative. In a subtle way, you were programmed to be attached to some emotions and resist others.

Today, whenever your mind notices an emotion, it springs into action by asking: *what am I feeling?* If it labels it as anger, sadness or fear, for example, then it will judge it as negative and want it gone. Unseen judgements happening in the mind are therefore a major hidden cause of emotional suffering and physical stress. So if you are ever struggling against a feeling, you can be sure there's been an unseen mind-based judgement that's decided it's bad, wrong or negative and a subsequent need for it to be gone for good.

There are no negative emotions, only some which feel less comfortable than others. Suspending judgement is therefore the antidote to any emotional suffering.

I am not suggesting never judging your emotions ever again because you can't necessarily stop your mind from judging things. However, I strongly recommend that you watch the judgements rather than be the judge. When you are the judge, you have identified with the commenting mind and become the judgemental thoughts. Enmeshed with the mind, you feel your thinking and it becomes very personal, with the inevitable consequence of getting caught further in thinking about how to feel better once again. However, when you can see the judgements from a more consciously aware viewpoint, you naturally step back from being the judge. The emotions stop being good or bad, positive or negative, and become a more neutral experience that you can calmly coexist with.

QUICK-START CURE:
COMFORTABLY UNCOMFORTABLE

To help you to cultivate being comfortable with uncomfortable energy, do the following quick-start cure:

1. Be consciously aware, by engaging GAAWO.

2. See the emotion don't be the emotion: observe the emotion instead of dropping into it.

3. See the judgement don't be the judge: observe the judgement thoughts happening in the mind.

4. Recognize the resistance and attachment: notice that for conflict to exist around how you feel, you are resisting one emotion and attached to feeling some other way.

5. Be in harmony with how you happen to feel: remaining aware, let the emotion be present.

More guidance on how to do this will be provided in Part III because it is a key skill in the Embodying Exercise. By seeing the emotion, instead of being the emotion; seeing the judgements about the energy, instead of being the judge; and being aware by engaging GAAWO, your feelings will be allowed to flow and find their optimum level. You will experience less mental struggle and physical stress, and your body will regain its energetic equilibrium, allowing for enhanced levels of health to emerge.

SUMMARY: UNCOMFORTABLE EMOTIONS

- It's natural to feel a full spectrum of emotional energies during your day-to-day life.

- Resisting your emotions creates stressful inner conflict.

- Suppressing emotions lowers your vital healing energy.

- Recognizing you have emotions but you are not your emotions can help you to calmly coexist with them all.

- All emotions are temporary, but your real Self is not.

- Peace is not the absence of emotions. Peace is a state of being you experience when you are consciously aware and at peace with however you happen to feel.

- Consciousness is calm. Peace is aware of all emotions.

- The more emotions the better because you need energy to heal, create and transform.

- Aim to feel your feelings without getting lost in them.

- See the judgements happening in your mind about the emotions instead of being the judge.

- To enhance health you need to be comfortable feeling uncomfortable.

SELF-HEALING STATEMENTS: UNCOMFORTABLE EMOTIONS

I am grateful for the emotional energy in my body.

I am happy that the energy is here to help me to heal.

I am the awareness that is aware of my emotions.

I am the peace that is aware of my emotions.

I am comfortable to sometimes feel uncomfortable.

Chapter 8

UNHEALTHY BELIEFS

The belief–body connection is real and relevant to your return to optimum health. Through my work with countless people from multiple continents, I've come to discover the power of the belief–body connection and observed several trends in the most common beliefs that appear to create disharmony and disease. When I first started out, I assumed self-limiting negative beliefs were the only culprits to compromised health. But on deeper examination, it was evident that a new definition for what in fact constitutes an unhealthy belief was necessary. Since stress is proven to be a key cause of ill health, I've come to the conclusion that any belief that causes stress can be deemed unhealthy. In this chapter, I reveal why beliefs are a secret source of stress and give guidance on how you can go beyond your beliefs to cultivate an inner mind–body climate conducive to physical healing, life-long wellness, satisfaction and success.

BRIEF BACKGROUND TO BELIEFS

Beliefs exist and operate in the unconscious mind, which is the realm that you are not consciously aware of. Working behind the scenes, beliefs determine the content of your conscious thoughts, justify the majority of emotions you feel, shape the actions you take and ultimately the life you end up living. Beliefs are formed via repetitive and significant events. Either you experience a series of similar events that cause you to come to a certain conclusion or you faced a singular emotional event that was so significant that your mind immediately generalized to form a belief.

For example, let's say at every family occasion a parent announced that you were 'the quiet one in the family'. Over time and through repetition, you could have taken on board the suggestion to form a belief. Or perhaps you got lost somewhere as a kid and found yourself full of fear. If it was significant enough, you could have formed a belief from that one event that always causes you to believe it's scary to ever be alone or separated from others.

You perceive what you believe.

Beliefs have such a big impact on your body and life because they are one of the main internal filters that influence how you perceive reality. Every moment you unconsciously take in a huge amount of raw data about your environment through your senses. The unconscious mind then makes sense of the data by editing it and attaching meaning. Due to this filtering process, your perceived version of reality is always unique and your relationship with yourself and life is governed largely by the collection of beliefs you've picked up along the way.

Perpetually finding proof that proves your beliefs

Although most beliefs are made at an early age, due to the way the mind operates, they can impact your body and life for decades. Whenever a belief is formed, your mind sets about proving it right. The filtering process deletes the data that's contrary to your beliefs and only makes you see, hear and feel the details that support what you believe. This is why your beliefs tend to feel so justified and true to you, to the point that if I were to say you have a problem with being alone because you have a negative belief about being alone, you may want to start telling me about all the times you have in fact been alone.

Or if I were to say you frequently feel stressed because of your belief system, you'd most likely want to list the times and things in your life that are in fact stressful. With the filtering process piling on more and more evidence to prove your beliefs to be true, it's no wonder you can get stuck in a particular mind-set. However, irrespective of whether or not you have a mountain of evidence to prove your beliefs right, if you want to benefit from Body Calm, I urge you to be open to new ways of perceiving yourself, your body and life in general.

THE BELIEF–BODY CONNECTION

Healing your unhealthy beliefs is paramount for self-healing. How you perceive life is going to impact how much stress your body endures. As a result, your beliefs have the potential of impacting many aspects of your body's physical functioning, including your immune system, blood pressure, cellular function and digestion. This makes logical sense, especially when you remember that the mind and body are intimately connected and the body experiences all that your mind perceives.

Body beliefs and stress beliefs

More specifically, I've observed two types of beliefs that can have a negative effect via the mind–body connection: Body Beliefs and Stress Beliefs. Body Beliefs relate directly to the messages sent between the mind and the body. Quite simply, the body follows the orders it is given. Examples of Body Beliefs include:

- I will gain weight the older I get.

- I always feel tired at the same times of the day.

- My eyesight will worsen with age.

- I always get the flu in winter or a cold in the summer.

Body Beliefs like these act as direct orders to the body, which it then sets about making true. Sickness brought on by our pre-programmed expectations is a phenomenon called the 'Nocebo Effect'. If, for example, you buy into the pharmaceutical-industry fuelled-belief that you always get the flu in winter, then your body will help to make it happen. Or if you believe you gain weight the older you get, then that, too, can become a self-fulfilling prophecy. When it comes to this second example, I'm writing from first hand experience.

When I was growing up, whenever my family went out for dinner, my mum would always say, with my best interests at heart, 'Sandy, eat whatever you want, but when you turn 30 you've got to watch out because you'll gain weight.' Well, guess what? I did eat whatever I wanted and within a couple of months of hitting 30, I noticed one day when sitting working at my computer, that I had, in fact, gained weight as my belly was resting on my legs! Thankfully, knowing what I'm sharing with you now, I was able to go beyond the belief and the weight dropped off, without me having to change my diet.

Although Body Beliefs impact the body, Stress Beliefs are by far the most influential upon health. They are the ones that cause you to enter into and stay stuck in an on-going state of stress due to some kind of inner conflict. Examples of these beliefs include: *I'm not safe, I'm not good enough, I'm not loved, I'm alone* or *I'm vulnerable*. Beliefs like these cause you to perceive yourself and your life in ways that create emotional tension, justify excessive thinking and lead to your body being in a perpetual state of fight-flight-freeze. But what makes these beliefs so stressful? This leads us to the new definition of what constitutes an unhealthy belief.

HIDDEN AT THE HEART OF UNHEALTHY BELIEFS

Despite stress being widely considered the most common cause of bad health, as I've already mentioned, I don't believe it is the ultimate reason why people get sick. This is because there is an additional element involved that must be happening for stress to exist, namely, conflict. Furthermore, for conflict to be present it requires the presence of opposing forces. In the context of unhealthy beliefs, this conflict again arises from the push-pull of resistance and attachment.

Resistance rejects, suppresses, fights, pushes away and puts pressure on the body. Resistance creates tension and tightness within the physical form that messes with the energetic equilibrium. It is also restrictive to optimum physical functioning. Although this sounds particularly bad, knowing this is very good news. It means stress is not caused by your circumstances, but by your resistance to your circumstances. The more you resist, the more stress your body endures.

Attachment, on the other hand, pulls, holds on, forces and controls, and again puts the body under pressure. Attachment is rooted in fear because it comes from a perception of need and separation. Attachment also buys into the illusion that you are incomplete without some externally sought addition. Beliefs born out of attachment will convince you that you need to find love from other people or you cannot be happy without the achievement of some kind of success, for example. The more attached you are, the more tense you will be.

Consequently, I define an unhealthy belief as any belief that justifies resistance and encourages attachment and leads to the inner conflict that's caused by their push and pull. This new definition makes for a very interesting investigation into which beliefs may be causing you stress. It stops being a battle between light and dark, positive and negative, limiting and empowering beliefs, and becomes more about determining which beliefs are causing you to be inwardly conflicted.

You see, a belief that may appear positive can in fact be causing you to resist and be attached, and therefore create stress within your body. For example, let's say you have a belief like, 'I am wealthy'. Upon first glance this appears to be a purely beneficial belief to possess. But what if the economy evolves, tastes change, people stop buying your products or services and you are no longer as wealthy as you once were? The positive belief of 'I am wealthy' can justify you resisting your current set of circumstances and be attached to keeping whatever wealth remains, in the process, leading to stress and ultimately ill health. To help your body heal, it makes sense therefore to go beyond any beliefs that justify you to reactively resist or be attached to your mind, body and life being any fixed way. With Body Calm, we do this by going beyond your beliefs all together!

All beliefs are limiting

In life, multiple outcomes are possible and what goes up will usually come down – eventually. As a human being, you will swing on the pendulum of possibilities. You will sometimes be positive, at other times lean towards the negative or hang out somewhere in between. However, if you believe you *must* stay at one side of the spectrum, there's going to be a part of you that is attached to one end and resistant to the other. This creates a conflict within yourself and limits your willingness to be something other than what you believe you must be. This way of living is fear-based rather than love-based and ends up being conditional and highly restrictive. By refusing to be any other way, you are going to resist regularly and harm your health.

Let's explore this with a few examples.

Resist	Attached
I am unloved.	I am loved.
I am unwanted.	I am wanted.
I am weak.	I am strong.
I am uncertain.	I am certain.
I am wrong.	I am right.
I am not enough.	I am enough.

What you resist persists

There is a tendency for people to want to be on the right side. By this, I mean to *only* be on the end of the spectrum where you *always* feel loved, wanted, strong, certain, right, enough, etc. However, if you are attached to being these things – and *only* these things – then there will inevitably be an inner conflict with attachment to the good side and resistance towards the negative. In reality, there are going to be times when you don't feel loved, aren't certain, or feel weaker than usual. Not accepting this possibility is the fast track to frustration and, believe it or not, makes it harder for your mind to accept the positive.

What you resist persists and what you don't want, you focus on, so it often comes towards you. It is very rare for anyone to find him- or herself in a state of absolute non-dualistic reality in which they *only* ever feel loved, wanted, strong, etc. Beliefs are therefore only ever relatively true because there is always the potential to experience the opposite, or something in between. Recognizing and being open to the entire spectrum leads to remarkable shifts. I've seen resistance reduce, attachments release and inner conflict clear – quickly – allowing for more inner calm and harmony with whatever happens. The end result is a freer and more fulfilled life.

Beliefs lose their power to cause conflict when you are willing to experience the full spectrum of possibilities.

Being willing to be all things is what makes the magic happen. Let's say you discover a belief like 'I am unloved'. One way to attempt to change it for the better would be to start thinking positive affirmations that represent the complete opposite, such as 'I am loved'. However, if you do that while still resisting the negative, there will remain an inner conflict that makes it harder for your mind to accept the new positive belief. You will also end up more inwardly conflicted. However, if you are willing to be both – unloved sometimes and loved at other times, then there is far less inner conflict and a heightened ability to embody ease. You will have less resistance to not being loved and you also won't be attached to being loved. You will find yourself less needy of love, which makes it easier for other people to love you and for you to feel it fully when they do.

Ultimately, you will discover that in your willingness to go beyond your apparently positive and negative beliefs, you can enjoy a huge amount of freedom in life.

TOP TIP: CLEAR THE CONFLICT

I'm not saying you should not be open to cultivating a positive attitude. I'm saying that if you are attached to *only* the positive then it can create inner conflict that will limit your self-healing capabilities. As you will have seen, the Body Calm meditation technique includes the use of positive statements called Body Calm Thoughts. The Calm Thoughts help you to heal the main negative beliefs because most people hold them more strongly than the positive. For example, one of the Calm Thoughts is 'I am enough' because I meet lots of people with illnesses who believe 'I'm not good enough'. To get the best from the Body Calm meditation technique, you need to ensure there is no inner conflict when using the Calm Thoughts. It is therefore highly recommended that you clear any inner conflict by exploring and applying what I'm sharing now.

FINDING YOUR STRESS BELIEFS

Let's turn our attention to you finding out what your unhealthy beliefs might be. Just because they exist and operate in your unconscious mind, it doesn't mean the evidence of them isn't in plain sight. To keep things simple, we will look in four main places: your thoughts, emotions, behaviours and body. For each, if you believe you've found a belief, then note it in a journal and use the quick-start cure shared at the end of the chapter.

Thoughts

The surface level of your mind can reflect your innermost beliefs. For instance, if you hold the underlying belief 'I am alone', then you will have more thoughts associated with trying to avoid being alone. If you believe 'I am vulnerable', then again, you will find the content of your mind mirrors that fear-based belief with thoughts about potential threats and the world being a scary place. For greater insight into your unconscious beliefs, your thoughts are a useful indicator.

Emotions

Beliefs justify the way you feel. Evidence of this is the fact that the same event can happen to two different people, but, if they have different beliefs, they will feel differently about it. Therefore, for greater insight into your beliefs, it helps to become aware of the most common ways you tend to feel. If you often feel unloved or unsupported or worthless, then there's a big chance you have beliefs that justify these frequent feelings.

Behaviours

How you act is also determined by your beliefs. If you believe that it's hard to make money, then you will filter out the easier avenues to abundance and focus your efforts on more effortful ways. If you believe you are always abandoned, then you will be more prone to behaving jealously because you have the subtle expectation of your partner leaving. Or if you believe you'll never meet anyone, you are going to end up acting differently around social situations and might even pull back from opportunities to form new or intimate relationships.

Body

Your beliefs become your body. If you want to know what your beliefs are then explore how your body is. If you believe you are fragile, then you body will be, too. If you have beliefs that make you inflexible, then your body will be prone to stiffness. Or if you believe people are a pain in the neck, well, you get the point! We will explore the symbolic nature of physical conditions more in Chapter 15. For now, the main thing to remember is that beliefs can be reflected within your physical form.

The most common stress beliefs

Having had the opportunity to work with hundreds of people to help them discover and resolve the beliefs impacting their health, I've observed themes in the most common negative stress beliefs, with some of the most prevalent being as shown below.

Stress beliefs	
I am alone.	I am unloved.
I am unsupported.	I am unwanted.
I am weak.	I am uncertain.
I am vulnerable.	I am stupid.
I am rejected.	I am wrong.
I am abandoned.	I am worthless.
I am bad.	I am insignificant.

I'm curious if any of the above listed beliefs feel true to you. If they do, I recommend using this quick-start cure.

QUICK-START CURE: BEING OPEN TO BEING BOTH

To reduce the power of a belief to create disharmony, you need to be willing to be both possibilities and everything in-between. Doing so resolves the resistance and appeases the attachment, collapses any inner conflict, reduces stress and helps the body to heal:

Step 1

Read through the following lists of beliefs and feel for whether you are resistant or attached to any of them. Remember, this may include some of the positive ones, too. They are unhealthy if they create inner conflict.

Perceived as negative	Perceived as positive
I am alone.	I am connected.
I am unsupported.	I am supported.
I am weak.	I am strong.
I am vulnerable.	I am protected.
I am unsafe.	I am safe.
I am rejected.	I am accepted.
I am abandoned.	I am cherished.
I am unloved.	I am loved.
I am unwanted.	I am wanted.
I am bad.	I am good.
I am uncertain.	I am certain.
I am stupid.	I am wise.
I am worthless.	I am valuable.
I am insignificant.	I am significant.

Step 2

Think or say out loud: 'All things are possible and I am open to being (state negative belief) sometimes and being (state positive belief) sometimes.' Then engage GAAWO and rest into the willingness of being both beliefs. Feel what it is like for both beliefs to calmly coexist as one experience within you. Then when you feel the shift has happened, take a deep breath in and out and open your eyes (if closed).

Don't worry, being willing to be both doesn't mean you will be more likely to hang out in the 'negative' side of the spectrum. Remember, it is your resistance to not being them that binds you to what you don't want. By resolving the resistance and attachment, you allow for a healthier relationship with your beliefs.

SUMMARY: UNHEALTHY BELIEFS

- Beliefs exist and operate in the unconscious mind.

- Beliefs are formed via repetitive and significant events.

- Beliefs are conclusions that you've come to based upon the information you have available at the time.

- Most beliefs are made early in life when you knew much less than you know now.

- The mind finds evidence to prove your beliefs right.

- Beliefs determine the content of your thoughts, justify the emotions you feel, the actions you take and the life you end up living.

- There are certainly positive and negative, empowering and limiting beliefs. Unhealthy beliefs are defined as those that create conflict due to the stressful opposing forces of resistance and attachment. Therefore a positive belief can in fact cause resistance and become unhealthy.

- Conflict is the hidden causes of stress.

- To increase health we must increase inner harmony.

- Being willing to be both 'positive' and 'negative' collapses the inner conflict.

- The Body Calm meditation technique works to heal the top 10 Stress Beliefs and in turn helps the body to heal.

SELF-HEALING STATEMENTS: UNHEALTHY BELIEFS

I am not the beliefs that I believe to be true.

I am the consciousness that is aware of my beliefs.

I am willing to let go of beliefs that do not serve me.

I am open to believing new things that help me to heal.

I am open to experiencing all possibilities.

Chapter 9

UNFORGIVEN PAST

Unforgiveness creates conflict that can hurt the body and hinder healing. With an unforgiven past you are resisting what happened while remaining attached to something more desirable happening instead. Although Body Calm is mainly a meditative approach focused on healing your relationship with your mind, body and life, when finding resolution with an unforgiven past, which could include some rather dark and difficult memories, it can be helpful to use a two-pronged approach:

1. Change your mind about the past by installing positive perspectives into negatively perceived memories.

2. Change your relationship with your memories about the past by being consciously aware of the present.

If you have gone through some challenging times, faced traumatic events and had things happen that you may feel very justified to judge as bad and resist to this day, your body and mind can sometimes need additional support, beyond meditation, to find complete closure. I've come to this conclusion having had the opportunity to work with people who I would consider to be very

Self-aware, having meditated for many years. However, despite their ability to be conscious, still, present and peaceful, by working to resolve emotionally charged events in their past, many have experienced significant improvements in their physical health. In this chapter I begin by giving guidance on how to forgive your problematic past events, before moving on to explore how my 'peace with' strategy can heal your relationship with any troublesome memories.

THE PARTS OF YOUR PAST PAUSED IN TIME

As I've already mentioned, everything happens to help you to fulfil your purpose of living fully and completely. This means that if you recoil from, reject or are overwhelmed by certain events, they are prevented from coming to completion. Imagine a line with the start point at one end and finish line at the other. If you have unforgiven past events, which still cause feelings of anger, sadness, fear, guilt, etc., it means you haven't yet arrived at the event's purposeful end point.

Unforgiven past events can remain active, even if you aren't actively thinking about the past anymore.

Despite life circumstances having moved on, it is like your unforgiven events have become paused in time. Due to the mind-body connection, as far as your body is concerned, incomplete events are *still* happening. If the events were particularly traumatic, then it means the red alert button has been switched on and your body has remained in a state of high alert ever since. As a result, events like these cause the body to be in a perpetual state of stress and they eventually end up harmful to health.

One of the common indications of this is talking about the past in the present tense. Other signs of an incomplete past include irritability, inappropriately high levels of emotional reaction to events that aren't that big a deal, a sense of something being processed in the background of your mind and certain memories always coming to mind when you are relaxing or wanting to get to sleep. Avoidance strategies are also often adopted when things are left unforgiven because they tend to bring up uncomfortable emotions if allowed to surface, leading to distraction tactics like needing the television or radio on to get to sleep, being addicted to being busy or habits such as emotional eating, to name a few.

If events remain unforgiven, then you remain in conflict with your past. The subsequent disharmony is detrimental to your health and happiness.

HEALING UNFORGIVEN EVENTS

Without the help of a time machine of sorts, you cannot change what's happened in the past. By this time in your life, you will have a multitude of memories, varied and ranging from the sublime to the ridiculous, the scary to the serene. Some you will be delighted to have enjoyed. Others you may hate having had to endure. Despite your current opinions, if health is what you really truly want, you must be willing to be at peace with your past.

Your body is the canvas. Your memories the paint.

Although you cannot change what's happened in your past, you can still create a masterpiece of memories that help you be a picture of health, for life. To do this, you must begin by letting go of wishing for a different past. Stop wasting your precious present moment trying to change a past that cannot be changed. Instead, turn your attention to the health-promoting task of being at peace with what happened, once and for all.

Resolving the root-cause conflicts

People get stuck in the past because they get caught up in the story *about* what happened. In doing so, they often go round in circles in their mind and instead of finding solutions, simply end up suffering. By trying to resolve the 'what' (i.e. the story about the event), they inadvertently remain one step removed from the real cause of why the event remains unresolved.

Moving to resolution requires you to withdraw your focus from *what* happened, to instead explore *why* you remain in conflict with what happened today. This is such a powerful shift in perspective because although you cannot change what happened, you can heal your inner conflict around any event. By healing the reason(s) why there has been an on-going disharmony, you become able to find resolution – irrespective of how bad the event happened to be. By clearing the conflict, harmony returns to the mind and body.

Conflict comes from the opposing forces of resistance and attachment. If any event remains unresolved for you, then it simply means you are subtly still resisting what happened and attached to something different happening instead. This push-pull dynamic will become very obvious when you start to explore your own unforgiven events. You will also notice it from now on whenever anyone else is talking about things in their life that they are in conflict with and are making them feel angry, sad, hurt, scared, guilty, etc. There will be elements that were unwanted (i.e. they resisted) and others that were needed (i.e. they were attached to). To find resolution, you need to be willing to reduce your resistance towards what happened and not need something different.

Life happens to elevate you into the
embodiment of enlightened living.

TOP TIP: THE EVIDENCE IS IN THE EMOTIONS

As a general rule, the emotion(s) you are feeling in relation to the past event(s) offer big clues as to what you are resisting and what you are attached to. You feel sad for different reasons to feeling angry or hurt or scared. So to clarify the conflict, begin by considering how it makes you feel. For example, guilt usually stems from a resistance to something you didn't do and an attachment to something you believe you 'should' have done differently. Anger and hurt are frequently due to a resistance to something that should not have happened to you and an attachment to something else that 'should' have happened instead. Whereas fear is often a survival-based resistance and an attachment to feeling more secure through certain criteria that were not met. Grief is a resistance to loss and an attachment to keeping what you believe you need to maintain the safer status quo. Although these are general examples, the principle remains true: To clarity your conflict, explore the emotions and track back to uncover the elements of the event you are resisting and attached to.

Remember, everything happens to help you. If you are resisting the past and attached to something different happening, then you haven't yet embodied the positive virtues that life was inviting you to become. To get the most from your past, be willing to perceive it from a positive perspective that enables you stop experiencing it as a problem now. The good news is this doesn't have to be hard or feel like a chore. In fact, it offers a wonderful opportunity for you to ease into a healthier mind-set and embody viewpoints and virtues that help you to accept the past and be an even wiser version of yourself today – one that would not have been possible without the events in your past.

With Body Calm you will start by considering more positive ways of perceiving past events. Making this shift can be the difference between life-long frustration-fuelled stress and life-changing serenity and freedom.

WHAT YOU KNOW NOW, YOU DIDN'T KNOW THEN

Unforgiven past events stay active because your mind is trying to find some kind of resolution. You were hurt or sad or scared and your mind wants to protect you from it happening again in the future. To help your mind return to rest, you need to give it some evidence that makes it know that it's safe to do so. For this, you are going to consider what you know now, which had you known in the past, you wouldn't have felt bad in the first place.

Evolve beyond thinking about past events as problematic with the help of hindsight and the wonderful wisdom you've gathered since.

Over the years, I've helped countless people find peace with the past. This has meant I've had the privilege of being present to hear all the wonderful wisdom that's led to the biggest 'aha' moments of their lives. I'm going to share seven of my favourites with you and have posed them as a series of questions to make them easier to relate to. They are incredibly powerful, yet be warned, they are also relatively simple, too. Often, people that have held onto memories for years will want to slap their foreheads for not realizing these revelations before now. This is quite common because most memories are from your younger life when you didn't know all that you know now.

The question is the answer

The trick for finding the best answer is to ask the right question. Consider the following seven questions and answers in light of your unforgiven events and notice how differently you feel by knowing them now.

1. Were you safer than you thought?

Consider this: *If you had known, for absolute certain, that you were going to survive the past event, how differently would you have felt at the time?* Feeling scared is often the result of our survival being uncertain. When clients are working with me to release past fears, they are often taking it for granted that they survived and are still here today to tell the tale.

By recognizing this simple truth that cannot be denied, the mind is able to turn off the red alert switch. Although you may not have liked what happened – even if some harm did come to your body – no longer fearing for your survival by knowing that you were safer than you thought at the time is a great start when seeking peace with the past.

2. What happened next?

The mind tends to dwell on the most traumatic parts of the past. In doing so it often neglects what happened next. For you to be reading this now, you can be sure it's not happening right now. In this moment you are reading this book and all is well again. I appreciate that the past event might have been tricky or painful to say the least. But I encourage you to cast your mind back to a point after the event when you were safe again and things were better. Taking account of this bigger-picture perspective, your mind will feel less justified to feel bad.

Meet Juliet, who healed a past racial attack

I once worked with a woman who had been racially abused in a subway tunnel as she walked home from school. Her root-cause conflict was 'scared I'm going to die' and when I met her she was very anxious and suffered with a compulsive cleaning disorder. When I enquired about what she remembered about the tunnel, she said there was dog dirt everywhere. I believe her mind had linked the feelings of fear with the dog dirt and over the years had generalized to make her feel uncomfortable around any form of dirt or mess.

When asked, What happened next? *She recalled going home, having dinner with her family and watching some television. After taking this on-board, when she thought back to the subway tunnel she felt calmer. Her mind had taken account of the fact that she would be OK and no longer felt as justified holding onto the fear. This also undermined the belief that her life was under threat. After the session she reported back that the need to compulsively clean had gone and she was now doing pottery lessons with her daughter; something she had never been able to do in the past because of her avoidance of dirt. (There's a video of Juliet's coaching experience with me on YouTube if you want to check it out.)*

3. Were you able to look after yourself?

As a baby you needed looking after. You were dependent on someone feeding you, cleaning you, clothing you and keeping you safe. Without them, you simply wouldn't have survived. However, times quickly changed and you have been able to look after yourself for much longer than you may be giving yourself credit for. This is a big thing to realize as many people hold onto anger, sadness, resentment or fear because they perceived a person wasn't there for them when they were growing up. This can lead to a subtle part of the mind *still* looking to be looked after today and a sense of underlying unease if support appears to be lacking.

If you are here today, able to read this book, then I can guarantee you were much more able to look after yourself than you may have previously thought. Yes, maybe you were left to your own devices at an age earlier than you felt was 'right', but don't let that distract you from the fact that you were very capable of looking after yourself and have been able to use your resourcefulness throughout your life to date. Knowing this can let you release your resistance and attachment around being looked after and feel more confident in your capabilities to be safe and secure.

4. Were the people dealing with their own stuff?

As children we also often view our parents and elders as gods. They knew and could do so much that we couldn't. Able to answer any question, they could pick you up in their strong arms, drive you places and even open any jar! It was only when we grew up to become adults too that we realized they were *only* human and had their own difficulties and stresses to deal with.

> *They shouldn't have known better because they couldn't have known better.*

Your parents didn't suddenly become enlightened and heal all of their stuff at the moment of your conception. Very much on their own journey of learning, evolving and embodying, they were and continue to be a work in progress, just like you. Maybe they could have been better parents; maybe they could have spent more time with you; or perhaps they could have been more loving. Irrespective of your opinions, they were doing their best in light of their own beliefs, emotional baggage, fears and limitations. By giving them a well-deserved break you naturally give your body a break from all the stress stemming from resisting how they were and the attachment to how you thought they should have been.

5. Did you take it more personally than you need to?

Another person's inability to be peaceful, happy or loving has absolutely nothing to do with you. Their actions are their side of the fence. Your reaction to their actions is your side. Their inability to love, for example, is something they need to evolve beyond, whereas your attachment to their love is something you need to learn how to let go of needing. Anything you are taking personally, you are usually neglecting within yourself.

Pointing the finger at people's faults misses a golden opportunity to let go of needing from them what you mistakenly believe is missing from inside you.

What you want is inside you. You don't need anyone to be any particular way for you to be well, peaceful or happy. Clean up your side of the fence by taking whatever they did less personally and focusing on what needs to be healed and embodied within yourself so their actions are not taken so personally. Your body will love the rest it gets from you learning to let go.

6. Have you been mind reading?

I'm constantly amazed by the years of heartache people can go through, when all the time their justification for feeling bad is based on a mind-read. The reality is most people don't even know what's going on in their own mind, so how are you going to accurately predict the innermost thoughts of someone else? Have you ever been cruel to someone you love? Have you ever pushed someone away who you really wanted to be close to? Or said things in the heat of the moment which you didn't really mean? If you've answered 'yes' to any of these, then how can you know for certain that if someone shouted at you or wasn't there for you, it must mean they didn't love or care about you? You can't.

Meet my dad, who hurt for half a century

My dad spent 50 years of his life feeling hurt because he believed his biological dad didn't love him. When he was very young, his dad left after returning from war, never to be seen again. Perhaps reasonably, he had assumed his dad didn't love him enough to stay and felt hurt by that 'fact'. Quite literally, half a century later, when his stepdad was on his deathbed, he was told to 'look everywhere' when clearing out the house.

Soon after his stepfather's death the unfortunate task of sorting through the house happened. As my dad was emptying the attic, he came across a book that turned out to be his baby annual, including photographs, poems and letters that had been sent and kept by his biological father. As he looked through the book, it became very clear that his biological dad had in fact loved him immensely. Furthermore, it dawned on him that his assumptions about why his dad had left had been wrong the entire time. Based upon a mind-read, he'd caused himself a lifetime of unnecessary hurt and heartache.

These days, my dad is one of the happiest people I know. For his sake, I wish he hadn't waited so long and I hope his story helps you to see beyond any mind-reads you may have made along the way. See the best in the people who you think have done you wrong. You can never know what they were really thinking. Even if they did say hurtful things, how can you honestly know if they meant it? You can't! Everyone wants to know peace, love and happiness, so it is safe to assume whatever gives your body the best rest and your heart the most happiness.

7. Were you not being very loving either?

One of the most common root-cause conflicts I come across relates to not being loved. With people presenting this perspective often feeling unloved because someone didn't act in a loving way towards them, was not there for them or not the parent or person that they wanted them to be. Without realizing it, through the resistance and attachment to someone else being different, they are not being very loving either.

The better you love, the better your body, naturally.

Love does not demand, it doesn't judge and it doesn't need anything to be different before it can be expressed. Love has no rules, conditions or requirements and does not include any hoops that need jumping through. So if you've felt upset because someone couldn't love you in the way you wanted, ask: *How loving am I being towards him or her? Did I want them to change? Have I been critical of their choices? Or am I resisting who they are, instead of loving them as they are?* Love lets yourself and others be enough, right now, knowing that everyone is doing their best and taking their own path home to the heart. I'm not saying you have to agree with all of their actions. Just love them in the knowledge that they've temporarily forgotten their real Self and that in their heart there is purity and goodness.

Cultivating compassion

When given the choice, I don't know anyone who doesn't want to be happy, peaceful and loving. It's what we all want, but our stuff can sometimes stand in the way. To get upset at someone for not meeting your expectations is to point the finger and say, *I'm angry at you for not knowing how to be happier, be at peace and experience love.* It's a bizarre thing to do. Nobody who is finding it hard to be happy needs your resentment. They want your love and acceptance, and so do you.

If in doubt or difficulty, ask: what would love do?

Forgiveness involves cultivating a more compassionate mind-set. Compassion is the combination of love and wisdom. To be compassionate is to see yourself and others through lovingly wise eyes. Instead of getting angry or hurt or getting down in the hole to suffer with another, you stay centred in your consciously aware Self. Remaining calm, observing without judgement and loving unconditionally, you become a living example that suffering is not necessary.

Compassion sees yourself and other people in their completeness – a perspective that only becomes possible when you are experiencing the fullness of your own perfectly whole and complete consciousness. From the still silence of the most aware aspect of your Self, you will find you no longer take things so personally or resist the actions of yourself or others. The motivation to mind-read is alleviated and you know deeply that everything happens to help you to live your purpose, and all is ultimately wonderfully well.

QUICK-START CURE: INSTALL THE NEW KNOWING

Within the context of an unforgiven past event, refer to the seven questions we've just explored and consider positive ways of perceiving an unresolved memory. Then use this exercise to install your new perspectives into your body–mind:

1. Ask: *Where do I know this in my body?* It's usually in the heart, chest, solar plexus or stomach area.

2. Ask: *If the knowing had a colour, what colour would it be?* Trust your first answer.

3. Keep that knowing there now.

4. With your eyes closed, use your imagination to go to the past, with the knowing, and play the movie of the old memory from start to finish, but this time, with the [*state colour*] knowing in your [*state location and learning*]. For example: *With the red knowing in my heart that I was safer than I thought.*

5. Once completed, bring the new knowing back to now by opening your eyes.

Example: Let's say you have an unforgiven event in which you felt unloved by an absent parent. You discover that you are resisting them leaving and are attached to their love. When exploring new ways of perceiving the event, you recognize that, although your parent wasn't there to love you, there were other people around that did. You were always safe and looked after. It wasn't personal that they found it hard to love you because they were dealing with their own stuff. And they simply didn't know how to show love to you and be there for you in the way you wanted. You would then ask yourself: *Where do I know all of this in my body?* Perhaps your heart comes to mind. Then ask: *If this knowing had a colour, what would it be?* Let's say the first answer you get is red.

You would then recall a memory when you felt unloved by your parent and play the memory from start to finish, but this time looking through the eyes of the younger you who has the red knowing in their heart that 'I was always loved, safe and looked after. It wasn't personal because my parent didn't know any better.' Then, once you feel the knowing is installed in the past version of yourself (which should take no longer than 30 seconds), come back to the present day by opening your eyes. Now, when you think about the memory or parent, you may find that the old negative emotions are gone and you feel at peace with what happened. This being the case, you will know that the conflict has been resolved and you are no longer resisting or attached to anything in relation to the past experience. Your body will thank you for the new found harmony with what's happened in your past.

PEACE WITH PAST MEMORIES

You may remember from the chapters on Body Calm Begins with Mind Calm and Uncomfortable Emotions that a primary aim of Body Calm is to get peace *with* your thoughts and emotions by being consciously aware. As memories are a type of emotionally charged thought, you can apply the same 'peace with' strategy to any memories that happen to pass through your mind too.

Memories range from events that occurred decades ago to more recent events from the past few minutes. It is natural to feel a range of emotions, depending on what happens during your life. I am not suggesting that you aim to become numb to life or never feel upset by challenging events. I also don't want you to feel like you can never think back to what's happened earlier. But to help your body to heal and stay healthy, you do need to reduce your time 'dwelling'.

Discover when you are dwelling

Dwelling occurs when you move from having a normal human reaction to the stuff that happens, to getting lost in the story and emotions about what happened, over a prolonged period of time. For example, let's say someone you love dies. It is human to feel upset. However, if you are still feeling upset weeks or months later, to the point that it's hurting your body, then it has become dwelling. Only you can know when you move from having a natural human emotional response to dwelling. As a general rule though, if you are suffering then you are dwelling. This is because, although the initial human reaction can be intense, it is a natural movement of energy and therefore no suffering is involved. But over time, if you are dwelling, you will be suffering from it due to excessive and prolonged thinking about it.

> *Your mind and body can't tell the difference between what's real or imagined.*

If you are lost in your mind, dwelling on incomplete memories, your body is going to end up repeatedly re-experiencing the trauma and stress of the thought-based memory. To avoid the resultant stress borne by your body, I recommend you engage GAAWO and let go of any memories you find yourself caught up in. (You can also use the full Body Calm meditation technique in Chapter 4 or the Embodying Exercise on pages 191–8) By becoming consciously aware, you step back from your entanglement in any particular memory to be able to observe from the serene sidelines of your real Self.

Although this may sound simple, I should highlight that it can sometimes be tricky. Memories can be emotional and feel very personal. They are about *your* life and you can feel compelled to think about them. So with this in mind, stay vigilant and recognize that if you want to give your body the best rest it needs to heal. Then, releasing your grasp upon your reminiscent mind is the wisest choice you can make. To let go of memories and get peace with your past, use this quick-start cure.

QUICK-START CURE: PEACE WITH THE PAST

If you ever do find yourself dwelling, then engage GAAWO and do the following:

1. See the memory, don't be the memory: observe the memory happening in your mind.

2. See the emotion, don't be the emotion: observe the emotions happening in your body.

3. Be in harmony with the memory: let the memory and emotion be present within you.

Don't push the memory away or try to pull a more positive emotion towards you. Be at peace with whatever is happening in your thoughts and emotions with the knowing that you are the calm consciousness that's aware of the mind and emotions. By no longer identifying with memories, they naturally fade away. By seeing the memory, instead of being lost in the memory; observing the emotions, instead of being the emotions; and being in harmony with the memory, your body will experience less stress and be more able to heal and to stay that way in the future. In summary, for inner harmony and healing, I recommend taking the advice of Robert Holden PhD, who at a recent Hay House conference suggested we embody the following simple yet powerful words.

'I forgive myself and the world... for everything.'

SUMMARY: UNFORGIVEN PAST

- Making peace with your past can help your body to heal.

- You can get peace with your past by installing what you know now into negatively perceived memories and by changing your relationship with memory thoughts.

- Unforgiven events remain active as though they are still happening and cause stress and disharmony due to you being in conflict with what happened.

- The body is the canvas. Your memories the paint. Although you cannot change what happened, you can still create a masterpiece of memories that help you to be a picture of health.

- Focus less on what happened and more on why you are still in conflict with what happened.

- Conflict comes from the opposing forces of resistance and attachment.

- Past events remain unresolved until you install new ways of perceiving them that mean there is no resistance or attachment.

- Life doesn't happen in order to hurt you, it happens to elevate you into the embodiment of enlightened living.

- If you feel bad about any past event, then it is incomplete and has not yet served its purpose.

- Explore new positive and love-based perspectives and then install them in your body–mind for harmony.

- Get peace with memories you are dwelling on by engaging GAAWO and making the present moment more important than the past.

SELF-HEALING STATEMENTS: UNFORGIVEN PAST

I am not my past. I am here and now.

I am the consciousness that is aware of my memories.

I am open to learning from my past.

I am open to new ways of perceiving my past.

I am grateful for every event in my life.

I am free from my past and excited about the future.

I am willing to forgive the world for everything.

Chapter 10

UNWANTED PRESENT

Being in conflict with your current life circumstances causes chronic stress, bad health and unhappiness. Although some aspects of your life may not be to your liking, if healing is what you really want, then it is paramount that you are willing to play with getting peace with your present. While contentment comes from letting 'what is' be enough, discontentment is encountered whenever you fall into the mind trap of believing you *need* more than what the present moment has to offer. You may notice I just used the word 'need' instead of 'want'. This is intentional because there's nothing harmful about wanting more from life and going for grandiose goals. Having a clear purpose that inspires you is highly beneficial for your health, vitality and longevity. It is when your intentions move from love to fear, desire to desperation and from want to need, that they create conflict with your current circumstances that plays havoc with your health and happiness.

In this chapter I will explore the mind-based causes and symptoms of an unwanted present and help you to return to harmony by exploring your realms of resistance and areas of attachment, before moving on to give guidance on cultivating courageous contentment and making the most of the magnificent moment.

WHY LIFE STOPS BEING GOOD ENOUGH

Growing up, you were taught what a good life looks like: the kind of houses you should live in, the makes of car you should drive, the holidays you should take and so on. With the best of intentions, the people you were around most during your younger years did their best to pass on the requirements for a happy and successful life. As the years rolled on, the advertising agencies and media organizations then jumped on the bandwagon to continue the conditioning. With the remit of convincing you that you didn't just want but *needed* their products or services, vast amounts of money have been invested in your materialistic indoctrination.

The American Dream

I'm writing this book while in the USA, which is known for the American Dream in which anyone who works hard can be successful, have a bulging bank account, drive a gas-guzzling car (or two) and live in a huge house surrounded by the proverbial white picket fence. Now don't get me wrong, I love the USA and the positive reinforcement that anyone can create the life of their dreams. However for millions of people worldwide the dream falls short, often ending up more of a nightmare because it perpetuates a massive amount of pressure to live up to superfluous societal standards that can take an enormous amount of time, effort and luck to achieve.

Believing you need your life to be filled with certain stuff *before* you can love it inevitably leads to the unnecessary postponement of contentment. It puts your perfect life at the end of the metaphorical rainbow. You never quite arrive at your idea of ideal because the goal posts keep moving with the advent of the next 'new and improved' thing that's a 'must have' for getting you 'there'. With your focus firmly upon the future, unsurprisingly you live in a state of angst and dissatisfaction, which is detrimental to the inner harmony that you need for health and true wealth.

*Happiness is uncaused, and welcoming whatever
you are given is the true generator of wealth.*

The downfall of the American Dream is due to the fact that you don't need any external possessions or prestige to be happy or to love your life. What you really want is inside you and can be found in this moment by being your real Self. This means that if your happiness and fulfilment is dependent upon external stuff, it will be forever temporary and founded on shaky ground. You will only ever be happy for fleeting moments when your life happens to meet your ever-changing needs, with discontentment quickly creeping in whenever things stop meeting with your hopes and dreams.

The comparison corroder

*Another fast track to frustration is comparing yourself
and your particular set of life circumstances with others.
Comparison corrodes contentment and leads to a sense of
lack, opening you up to inner conflict and disharmony with
your current lot. The reality is, we live in a world of class
systems, ever-widening wage brackets and unequal access
to material wealth and resources. As a result, there's an
extremely high chance that some other person on the planet
is going to be able to have bigger and better things than you.
During your lifetime this may always be the case, irrespective
of how much personal wealth you manage to accumulate or
how strong your personal buying power becomes.*

'Keeping up with the Jones' is therefore a mind trap that you need to no longer get caught up in. At the root of comparison is the mind-based habit of judgement. In its desire to find your position in society, your mind may always default to judging whether who you are and what you have is better or worse than others. If, based on your beliefs and conditioning, your mind decides that what you have is worse, then you can quickly become discontented, not because you have less than someone else, but because your mind has deemed what you have as not good enough. The natural knock-on effect of the subsequent resistance and attachment to needing something different is an abundance of conflicted emotions. Most likely you will end up feeling sad, jealous, frustrated or apathetic, lowering your vital healing energy levels and health in the process. This is not good for your body and certainly not helpful for your happiness. Learning to be content is therefore a genuine 'must have', if you want to bring your body back to balance and enjoy true health and wealth, for life.

RESISTANCE TO RECOVERY

Having identified the symptoms of an unwanted present, let's dive deeper to explore the potential causes of your discontentment. To do this you are going to explore your realms of resistance and areas of attachment. Remember, for there to be conflict with your current reality and therefore disharmony, the forces of resistance and attachment are going to be present.

Realms of Resistance

In relation to your current life circumstances, *What are you resisting? What don't you want? What are you pushing away? What do you want rid of and out of your life for good?* Although you may feel justified in not wanting these things, that's not the point. What's more important is to recognize that it's not these things, but your resistance to them, that's causing your lack of contentment at the current time. By highlighting them, you make a big step towards no longer unintentionally being a victim to circumstance. They are not the cause of your dissatisfaction; it's your resistance that is. Although you may not be able to make immediate changes to your situation, you can choose not to resist them. To help, here are a few examples of the kinds of things you may be resisting. If you recognize yourself in any of them, take note and use the Courageous Contentment Quick-start Cure on pages 143–4 to release the resistance and return to harmony with 'what is'.

Realms of Resistance	
Health	Are you resisting pain, discomfort and itchiness or bloating? Are you resisting a diagnosis or not knowing if you will heal? Are you resisting not being able to do the things you want because you have a physical condition?
Relationships	Are you resisting your partner's looks, opinions, beliefs, values or habits? Are they not doing what you want or showing you love in the way you want it? Is a family member, friend or colleague not behaving how you want? Are they needy or demanding of your time or attention? When you think of your relationships, which one comes to mind as being problematic? What about the relationship do you not like?
Career	Are you resisting your current career path? Do you find it repetitive, boring or uninspiring? Do you dread the daily commute or hate being away from your family? Are the deadlines difficult or is the workload heavy or do you dislike the place? Is the pay bad or is the job security tentative? Do you wish you were doing something different but feel stuck where you are?
Money	Are you resisting your current bank balance? Do you struggle to pay the bills, hate counting your cash and wish you were better off? Are your investments underperforming or have you lost money in bad deals? Are you in debt, have a mortgage to pay off or stuck with property or possessions you want to sell but they aren't budging?

(continued)

Realms of Resistance	
Environment	Are you resisting your current living and working environment? Do you wish you lived somewhere else? Do you hate the cold, rain, sun or heat? Do you wish you could work from home, never go back to the office or travel less or more? Does your house need updating or are home improvements taking longer than you had hoped?

Just because you aren't resisting, it doesn't mean that you cannot make a positive change. It only means you will no longer mentally, emotionally and physically suffer as a result of the reactive resistance. What you resist tends to persist, so if you do want to improve things, then coming from a place of inner contentment is the ideal platform from which to proceed.

Areas of Attachment

In relation to your current life circumstances, *What are you attached to? What do you believe you need that you don't currently have? What are you trying to pull towards you? What do you want to keep and have in your life forever?* Although you may feel justified in wanting them, again, that's not the point. What's more important is to recognize that it's not these things, but your unseen attachment to them, that's causing any discontentment. By becoming aware of them, you can choose to no longer postpone feeling good until after you get them. Remember, they are not the cause of your dissatisfaction; it's your attachment to them that is. Although you may or may not be able to get what you think you need, you can choose to not need them and in turn, return to a more rested mind and body.

To help, here are examples of the kinds of things you may be attached to at the current time. If you recognize yourself needing any of them, take note and use the Courageous Contentment

Quick-start Cure on pages 143–4 to appease the attachment and let 'what is' be enough.

Areas of Attachment	
Health	Are you attached to making your body be a certain shape or weight? Or look a certain way? Do you wish you had a slimmer body, smoother skin, less cellulite, no pimples or scars? Do you wish you were taller, shorter, prettier or more handsome? Will you not be happy or feel confident until you've changed something about your body? Are you attached to a physical condition getting better, or to living longer?
Relationships	Are you attached to a particular person in your life? Do you need your partner to speak to you, look at you or touch you in a specific way? Are you attached to meeting someone new and being in a relationship? Are you attached to people thinking about you positively and being liked?
Career	Are you attached to your career? Will you not be happy until your career changes? Do you need job security or wish you were made redundant? Are you attached to getting a promotion or being recognized for the work you do? Are you waiting to be happy when you retire?
Money	Are you attached to money? Do you need a certain amount in your bank account to feel confident and secure? Are you attached to your investments doing well? Will you not be happy until you've paid off your credit cards or mortgage? Are you attached to your possessions to the point that you worry about losing them?

(continued)

Areas of Attachment	
Environment	Are you attached to living or working in a specific environment? Will you not be happy until you've moved, emigrated, left home or moved back home? Are you attached to working from home or do you need something to improve at your office or workplace? Will you only be happy when you've done some DIY, got a new kitchen or carpet or made some other home improvement?

Let me repeat, I'm not asking you to give up on your goals. Attachment occurs when you move from love to fear, desire to desperation and want to need. The interesting thing about fear, desperation and need is that they tend to push away what you want to bring towards you. These low level mental and emotional states act as repellents, often making it harder for you to attain what you want. Acknowledging your attachments like this and then being willing to let them go is therefore key to making improvements and getting your goals. We've all heard about the people who meet their life partner when they finally start enjoying being single and let go of ever being in a relationship. The same law of attraction works here. Know what you want, but let go of needing it.

THE PRESENT THAT KEEPS GIVING

Perhaps ironically, the ultimate cause of an unwanted present is *not* being present. When you withdraw your attention from the now, you enter into a world of lack, limitation and separateness. You end up in your head thinking about life instead of directly experiencing it. One step removed from the moment you're in, your thoughts about life are empty and shallow compared to the deep fullness of the multi-sensory, rich and real present moment.

*When attentive to now, you are aware of
all that is being presented to you now. And
there is always so much happening!*

At the sensory level, there are a multitude of colours, textures, shades and shadows. There is an abundance of sounds and a host of physical sensations and kinaesthetic curiosities. So much so that, when your attention is filled with 'all that is' now, it's near impossible to experience anything less than completeness and contentment.

Conscious awareness is the doorway to the kingdom of calm that is the present moment. When you are consciously aware you are gazing out from the aspect of your Self that is always present. You see, consciousness is only ever aware of what's being presented to it now. Awareness is the eyes of the watcher and the ears of the silent listener. Yes, you can place your attention on your thoughts about the past and the future, and get the impression that you aren't present. But the reality is, the awareness that's aware of your time-based thoughts is only ever aware of the thoughts that are happening now. It is simply aware of wherever your focus happens to be.

This means that if you rest into your conscious awareness by engaging GAAWO, for example, then you naturally and immediately experience the present. You align your attention with your awareness and directly experience consciousness. Automatically, you also experience what your conscious awareness feels like, which, if you're exploring it for yourself, you'll know is calm, still, silent and spacious. By being present and experiencing your Self, you can discover that you are already perfect, whole and complete, and need nothing external. No person, possession or prestige is required for you to be enough or have enough and you need do nothing to inherent the richness of reality. Be your Self by being still now.

There are no present moment thoughts. All thoughts are about the past and future, even ones about now.

Thinking about the present isn't *being* present, so watch out for the subtle mind trap. When I first heard about the importance and benefits of being present, I didn't know how to be consciously aware like you do. So I thought being present was thinking about what was happening now. I would think to myself, 'OK, so I'm here, and I can see a tree and I can feel my feet on the ground and, wait, what's that sound...?' Although I had the best of intentions, I still wasn't present. I was just thinking thoughts about the moment. Being present requires no on-going commentary about what's happening. Engaging with the commentator just keeps you separate from now because you remain one step removed from the moment, in your mind. The easiest and most effective way to be present is to be consciously aware. As an added benefit, when you are conscious, you naturally get peace with your present. No longer governed by the critical judgements of your mind, you can discover that the only way to have a problem with the present is to leave it by thinking about it.

Conscious awareness has no opinion. Remember the sky and birds analogy I shared earlier? The sky doesn't care what birds are flying around within it. Similarly, consciousness doesn't care what it's aware of. It just allows everything to come and go while remaining untouched and unconcerned by any of it.

Consequently, getting peace with the present requires you to get peace with the thoughts you are having *about* the present. While remaining consciously aware, observe the thoughts happening in your mind, without engaging in them. If you can remain aware, you will enjoy the serene stillness of your consciousness, even if you're having negative thoughts, and you will experience what it's like to be calm *and* have thoughts simultaneously. This is 'peace with mind' and when you have peace with mind you will enjoy the love-filled liberation of having 'peace with life', too. This means you are well, irrespective of what happens in your thoughts, emotions, body, relationships, career, finances, environment and every other aspect of your human experience you can name.

Fully attentive to now and filled up by the multi-faceted moment, your awareness is wide open and taking in all that is, right now. Naturally you no longer identify or engage in any one thing. Nothing is more or less important than the other. With this, thoughts and emotions stop being the sole focus of your attention, they are just parts of the greater whole. Like stars in the night sky, dots in infinite space, they become smaller and, as a result, stop having such a big impact. They may continue to happen, but because they are no longer all that you are aware of in any given moment, you are peacefully living with them. Wow! This inner shift is the key to freedom from problems and living fully and completely. I urge you to explore it in your own life; the positive possibilities are truly infinite!

QUICK-START CURE: COURAGEOUS CONTENTMENT

This quick-start cure is called 'Courageous Contentment' because it can take courage to be contented. Few people are willing to let their life be enough. Over the years you've been taught to need certain things to be happy and conditioned by the media to have an unquenchable thirst for more. It is my hope that, by now, you are seeing the abundant benefits of investing in the cultivation of contentment. When it comes to learning how to be contented, less is more. Enough is enough, after all. With this in mind, recall the realms of resistance and areas of attachment we explored earlier. From the lists offered or using ones you came up by yourself, do the following:

1. For resistance, think silently or say aloud: I can prefer to not want this without pushing it away.

2. For attachment, think silently or say aloud: I can want this without needing it.

3. Then engage GAAWO and consider the following: What is my inner experience like when I let this moment be enough, exactly as it is?

4. If you engage letting this moment be enough, there will be a calm, contentment and completeness within you.

SUMMARY: UNWANTED PRESENT

- Being in conflict with your current circumstances causes chronic stress, bad health and unhappiness.

- Contentment comes from letting now be enough.

- Discontentment happens when you resist 'what is' and believe you need more than what the present moment has to offer.

- Having inspirational goals is beneficial to your health, vitality and longevity.

- Goals become unhealthy when your intentions move from love to fear, desire to desperation and from want to need.

- Growing up your materialistic indoctrination conditioned you to think you always need more.

- Comparison corrodes your contentment, so be aware of whenever you fall into that common mind trap.

- Move from resistance to recovery and reduce your realms of resistance by accepting that you can prefer to not want things without pushing them away.

- Appease your attachments by recognizing you can want things without needing them.

- Perhaps ironically, the ultimate cause of an unwanted present is *not* being present.

- Be here, now, by being consciously aware of your real Self to have peace with your present moment, freedom from problems and live fully and completely.

SELF-HEALING STATEMENTS: UNWANTED PRESENT

I am content with my current life.

I am in harmony with what happens.

I am excited about my goals without needing them.

I am free to want more and let what I have be enough.

I am the awareness that is aware of now.

I am at peace with my present moment.

Chapter 11

UNLOVED BODY

Fighting your physical form is counterproductive to your body being in balance and you benefiting from brilliant health. If you are engaged in a battle with your body, it is tiring and creates feelings of unfairness and frustration. Also, when your body is presenting physical discomfort, not functioning as you want, and limiting your life choices and enjoyment, it is common to feel like your body is acting against you. However, in my observation, the body is working in quite the opposite direction.

Body Calm comes from befriending the body. I've discovered that a healthier relationship with your body is fundamental and built upon two foundational shifts in awareness. Knowing these can totally transform how you relate to your body and enable you to experience a sense of calm and contentment that helps healing and is not dependent upon how your body happens to be. In this chapter I reveal these two key principles and provide guidance on how to apply them to your mind and body.

AWARENESS 1: MY BODY IS NOT AGAINST ME

Due to the immaculate mind-body interconnectedness, your body is constantly responding and adapting to the mental and emotional climate in which it exists. With the prime objective of surviving, it does everything it can to sustain life. Now I accept this may not always appear to be the case, especially if it looks like your body is malfunctioning, feels faulty or is heading in the direction of its own demise. However, if you take on board that your body is not against you, then you can be in a better position to understand why it's doing what it's doing and help it to function how you want.

To sustain life the body adapts to survive.

Believing your body is broken also tends to lead to the assumption that you need to look outside yourself to get fixed. You inevitably turn to a lotion, potion, pill or operation to find relief and resolution. However, if you know your body is adapting to survive, then you naturally look within your own mind and life to find the possible causes of the conditions and the solutions to your symptoms. Combine this with the understanding that your body becomes whatever you're thinking about the most. It's no longer the fault of your genes, you haven't caught it, and it's not down to wear and tear or simple bad luck. You consider the possibility that your body is mirroring something in your mind and life, and your physical form has cleverly adapted as a result of the intention to survive.

Physical conditions are no longer so troublesome, but an opportunity to make positive changes to your mind and life that are aligned with your higher good.

> ## TOP TIP: LESS HEALING, MORE ADAPTING
>
> Understanding this principle can also help you change your relationship with 'self-healing' in general. The term 'healing' can be an emotionally charged one with many negative associations. The prospect of having to 'heal' yourself is a daunting task for many and through our conditioning we can be programmed to believe we cannot do it without pharmaceuticals or operations. Again, I'm not saying you shouldn't turn to modern medicine, but that you do so alongside complimentary means. So instead of using the term 'healing', it is useful to swap it for 'adapting'. Your body has adapted to create the condition and, given the right inner climate, will adapt again, back to health.

Assume that your body has your back

Think of your body, as your life-long friend who's doing its best to keep you safe and encourage you to live fully and completely. Knowing your body is on your side, you ask better questions. Instead of feeling a victim you know your body is on your side and ask: *What is my body trying to tell me with this physical condition?' What in my life is causing my body to adapt to help keep me safe? How might my body be mirroring something in my mind or life right now?*

Some examples of the body adapting to survive

Let go of any labels you may have picked up to define the condition or concern and do your best to distil your description down to what exactly the body is physically doing. For example, with 'psoriasis' the body is creating an extra thick skin or with 'constipation' the body is holding on. To help you move into a more inquisitive mind-set for understanding the different ways the body adapts to survive, let's explore some examples that have come from my observations during clinical practice:

Psoriasis

The body is creating an extra thick skin. The skin is the external line of defence. Commonly, people I meet with symptoms of psoriasis are feeling under attack, bullied or have unresolved past events that have caused them to fear for their survival. To explore this, you could ask: *Why might my body believe it needs to create a thicker skin? Who have I felt, or do I feel, bullied by? Where in my life do I feel threatened or under attack?*

Constipation

The body is holding on and/or not letting go. Very often people who want my help to heal constipation are attached to someone or something in their life and/or resisting letting go. A loved one may have died and the person is still mentally and emotionally attached to them. Or they are scared about or resistant towards losing someone or something important to them. For instance, this may also include worrying about losing a pet, a home or a job. Or they may have concerns around not having enough money for example, which is making them hold on to the limited funds they've got. Overall, their body is reflecting the tendency to hold on and/or not let go. To investigate this, ask: *What am I holding onto? What am I not willing to let go of? What am I worried about losing? What's happening in my mind or life that would make my body hold on?*

Headaches

The body is creating pain in the head. It is common for people with headaches to have something on their mind. It is usually linked with anger and/or guilt towards themselves, which at some level makes them feel deserving of punishment in the form of pain. Intense headaches and migraines tend to also encourage hiding away, turning the lights off and shutting life out by closing the eyes. To explore this, ask: *What's been playing on my mind? What's happened in my life that I feel anger or guilt towards myself? What in my mind or life do I want to hide away from or get away from?*

Fatigue

The body is lowering its energy levels. It is common for people presenting fatigue to have a situation in their life that they feel they have failed to fight or can't stand up to. They've also tried to 'flight' by running away, but feel stuck and unable to get away. So the body has turned to the third way of protecting itself by freezing i.e. playing dead. One way it does this is by reducing energy levels. Retreating to rest with the intention of getting away from the past or present person or situation is therefore a common cause of fatigue. To explore this, ask: *What have I been struggling against in my life over a prolonged period? What in my life have I not faced up to or got away from? What stressful situation(s) do I feel stuck with?*

These are a handful of quick examples to illustrate the incredible ability of the body to adapt to the emotional and environmental conditions that it encounters. I will share more common conditions and causes in the chapter When the Body Speaks. But for now, within the context of befriending your body, I hope you are beginning to appreciate the stunningly symbolic ways in which the body changes to help you stay safe and sustain life. Even if you aren't yet aware of exactly why your body may be adapting to survive or what's caused your current condition, you can still start benefiting from the positive side effects. For this, let's harness the power of the self-healing states of praise, gratitude and love.

Learning to love your body

What you resist persists, so the more you battle with your body, the less likely it is that positive changes will occur. Having an attitude of gratitude towards your body is key to healing your relationship with your physical form.

*The antidote to annoyance is appreciation
and the first step to love is praise.*

If I were to ask you to be thankful for your body it might be hard, mainly because you probably don't want the current condition(s) it suffers from and there may be things you don't like about it. To get around this, I'm going to invite you to play with praising your body instead. By praise I don't mean anything religious. To praise is to make it a priority to look for what's right instead of what's wrong and what's good rather than bad. Praise is powerful. But I'm going to wait to share why, until after you've experienced the power of praise for yourself.

Starting with something non-body related I invite you to find something that you do not like in the location where you are currently reading this book. I appreciate this may be a rather odd request, especially in light of the rest of this book. But just for now, please find something you don't like in the space in which you are currently residing. Now, having found it, I want you to actively criticize it in your mind for no longer than 15 seconds. You have permission to be negative while you genuinely criticize whatever you've found in your locale that you don't like.

Now, how does it feel? If you fully engaged the exercise, you will have observed your energy drop, emotions dip and may have even noticed a tightness, heaviness or tension within your body, usually in your chest or stomach areas. I'm sure you will agree it's not very nice!

First, this demonstrates the mind–body connection in action. However, the point I want to make requires part two of the process. Now, with the exact same object or thing that you were previously thinking negatively about and criticizing, I want you to find a few things to praise about it. To do this you may have to dig deep and be creative, but please do your best. Find and think about a few things that you can praise for up to 15 seconds. Perhaps you found a stain on the carpet. To praise it you would praise the fact that you have a carpet that keeps the place warm. Or maybe you saw a painting on the wall that you don't like. To praise it you might consider how someone has taken the time to find the paint and canvas and create some art, it's been put in a picture frame and then hung on the wall to bring colour to the room. Irrespective of what you're working with, take a few moments to actively praise it now.

How did you get on? How do you feel now? Has your energy improved, emotions lifted and does your body feel more relaxed? If you were sincere with your praise, I guarantee you will be feeling better – mentally, emotionally and physically. So what's the point of this praise game? It boils down to the simple fact that the thing you were criticizing and praising didn't need to change for you to feel better and for your body to become more relaxed and get some rest. Praise is so powerful because it is something you can choose to do, and when you do, it causes immediate improvements. The implications of this are huge when it comes to befriending your body and helping your body to heal. I'm not saying any physical condition will have been cured in the past three minutes, but your body will be in a better state. Ultimately this simple exercise proves that your body doesn't need to change or heal or be different in any way whatsoever before you can feel better and your body benefit from accessing a more restful state.

With the power of praise you can feel good now and in the process be friendlier to your body.

Now find something you don't like about your body. By doing so, you will most likely instantly fall into a negative commentary and judgement of it. As your body and emotions follow the mental activity, you will find it doesn't feel nice to think about. Now, using the same skill you just learnt, find something to praise about the aspect of your body that you don't like. You might need to be creative and think outside the box, but do your best. Actively think about what you can praise. Let's say you have a skin condition. You could praise the fact that you have skin! That it is waterproof and protects you against pathogens while also regulating your temperature, synthesizing vitamin D and enabling you to experience touch with as many as 2,500 receptors per cm^2 on the fingertips alone. Pretty amazing really, to have skin! You'll know you're doing this exercise right because you will feel upbeat and inwardly rested where there was once tension. Try it and see how your relationship with your body becomes more loving.

Praise leads to gratitude and gratitude leads to love

Remember earlier how I said it might be a 'big ask' for me to tell you to jump straight into loving your body? The good news is you don't have to when you make praise a priority. Quite magically, you will discover very naturally that praise leads to gratitude and gratitude leads to love – with the combination of praise, gratitude and love being compassion. So if in the past you've found it hard to love your body, you now have a key to open the door to not only befriending your body, but also to loving it, too.

When you choose praise over criticism, you find reasons to be grateful, loving and compassionate. Compassion has been found to almost double certain aspects of the immune system and help the body heal more quickly.[1] Due to its positive impact upon the coherence of the heart rhythms, gratitude has the potential of having a positive knock-on effective with many of the other essential organs, too. Furthermore, as you develop an attitude of gratitude, you will find yourself falling back in love with your body (and yourself). The healing by-products of love are immense, with love being documented in scientific studies as helping restore the nervous system, giving pain relief, supporting cardiovascular health and even being a key factor in living longer.[2] In short, there are so many physical benefits from the emotional states of gratitude and love that it makes befriending your body an absolute must. So before moving on to the next shift in awareness, please set the intention to regularly meditate upon or say out loud these self-healing statements, as they will help you to embody what you've learnt.

SELF-HEALING STATEMENTS

Thank you body, for allowing me to experience life.

Thank you body, for adapting to keep me alive.

Thank you body, for healing so that I may be healthy.

Thank you body for all the wonderful work you do.

Thank you body, for being my friend during this life.

AWARENESS 2: I AM NOT MY BODY

Having an appreciation of your body working in your best interest is part of befriending it. Cultivating Body Calm goes further by encouraging you to have a potentially radical new relationship with your physical form, too. Although you have a body, you are not your body. Your body is temporary and changes, but there's an aspect to you that is permanent and has remained unchanged since before you were born, an aspect of you that stays unaffected, even if something bad happens to your body. Consider this: *If you were to accidentally lose the end of your little finger, would you lose part of your Self or lose a bit of your body?* The reality is you may have a part of your body missing, but *you* would be fully intact. The 'you' I'm referring to, is the aspect of you that is beyond the physical form. It is the non-physical, presence of your conscious awareness.

Earlier in the book I asked the rather curious question: *How do you know you have a body?* The answer is, you know you have a body because you are aware of it. By that rationale, there is a physical aspect of you, your body, and a non-physical part, which is your consciousness. The consciousness that is aware of your body is the constant and unchanging element of you and it pays dividends to get to know it well, if you want to totally transform how you relate to your body. As long as you are your body, you are vulnerable and separate. Your mood will also be fully dependent on what happens within your health and if your body presents physical symptoms, you will end up suffering as a result. Consciousness on the other hand is unbreakable. It is a peaceful presence that, to date, no evidence exists about to suggest it dies when the body does. Get to know your own consciousness and you can discover the timeless and immortal nature of your real Self.

The body is the temporary home for the eternal consciousness that is your real Self.

Being the awareness that's aware of your body

Being consciously aware connects you with your real Self. As a natural by-product, it becomes very obvious that you are not your body, leading to the realization that your consciousness never gets sick and is perfect, whole and completely calm, now and always. Remarkably, you don't fear death, which is incredibly liberating. Neither do you have to wait for your body to heal before you can access and enjoy stunning states of being, like peace, love, joy, contentment and freedom. Naturally, you can calmly be with any physical issue.

Within the context of self-healing, knowing you are not your body is therefore paramount. By being calm now through being attentive to your permanently present conscious awareness, your body is subjected to far less stress. By calming your busy mind, your body also benefits from improved communication within the body and mind. Instead of it being bombarded by a host of angst-mongering negative thoughts and emotions, there exists an inner climate of calm and clarity. Your body experiences superior levels of rest during the day (and night) and performs its maintenance and repair projects. Sound exciting? One of the purposes of the Body Calm meditation technique is to help you to discover and rest within your conscious awareness. By engaging GAAWO and using the Calm Thoughts you get to know and experience an inner, still, silent presence and when you do, you experience your real Self. This is because still, silent calmness is what consciousness feels like. To help you to rediscover your Self, beyond your body, I invite you to use this Booster Calm Thought during your Body Calm meditation practice.

BOOSTER BODY CALM THOUGHT: 'I AM'

You may remember from earlier when learning the Body Calm meditation technique (see Chapter 4) that 'I AM' refers to the aspect of your Self that is unconditioned consciousness. As such, it is beyond your body, personality traits or anything else that may be self-limiting or stress inducing. Consequently, it is immensely powerful to think 'I AM' on its own. When doing your Calm Sittings, if once you've used all 10 Calm Thoughts you wish to continue meditating longer, use the following Booster Calm Thought:

I AM (focus point: UNCONDITIONAL LOVE)

The focus point for this Booster Calm Thought is different to the rest. With 'I AM' you place your awareness on unconditional love. This is a more advanced Calm Thought because it may not make complete sense, initially. But if you use it with an open mind and heart then you will find beautiful benefits can be gained. You aren't going to think 'unconditional love' (although don't worry if it pops into your mind), instead, just get a sense of it. In my opinion, the belief that you are separate from love sits at the core of conditioning, fuels fear, perpetuates the sense there's 'something wrong' with you and your life and is a major cause of disharmony, stress, emotional suffering and ill health.

Thinking 'I AM' with your awareness on unconditional love has the power to close the gap between your sense of Self and the presence of love. The closer you come to knowing your Self as love, the more in harmony your heart, mind, body, soul and life naturally become. Play with it and enjoy the boundless benefits of being intimate with the presence of your being – that is love.

Unifying your sense of self with unconditional love is the purpose of this Booster Calm Thought.

SUMMARY: UNLOVED BODY

- Your body is never working against you.
- Your body is adapting to survive the mental, emotional and environmental climate in which it exists.
- Your body is a mirror of your mind and life.
- Whatever your mind consistently thinks, feels and perceives, your body becomes.
- Use the power of praise to fall back in love with your body.
- Body Calm requires a new relationship with your body.
- Although you have a body, you are not your body.
- The body is the temporary home for the eternal consciousness that is your real Self.

- Being consciously aware helps you to experience that you are not your body.

- You don't have to wait for the body to heal to be calm.

- Consciousness is perfect, whole and calm, always.

- Through disengaging the thinking mind by experiencing your conscious awareness, you can calmly live with your body and any physical condition.

- The calm that comes from being consciously aware helps the body to heal due to lowered stress levels and improved communications within the body–mind.

SELF-HEALING STATEMENTS: UNLOVED BODY

I am supported by my body, which wants to be well.

I am the consciousness that is aware of my body.

I am always well, even when by body is healing.

I am at peace with however my body happens to be.

I am grateful for the home of my harmonious being.

Chapter 12

UNHEARD HEART

Returning to radiant health requires you to be heroic by listening to and living in agreement with your heart. Your heart knows the truth of who you are, what's right for you and what your life purpose is, and wants you to walk fearlessly and selflessly in the direction of your dreams. However, losing connection with your real Self has the hidden by-product of you not being able to properly hear your heart's guidance. Or, if you do hear it, you can let fear stop you from taking action on its advice, often leading to getting stuck in situations that are wrong for you, which over time causes conflict, suffering and stress. Due to the disharmony within your heart, mind, body and soul, an unheard heart is by far one of the most common causes of unhappiness and compromised health.

Your heart is constantly communicating via your intuitions, silent knowings and frequent feelings.

Listening to your heart is a heroic act because it requires you to trust and act upon your inner knowing(s) instead of letting logic or fear get the better of you. If you don't listen, then life becomes limited and compromised, which is corrosive to both your health and happiness. Moreover, the less you listen to your heart, the more your head ends up driving things. Head-centred living makes you more inclined to operate from ego-based selfishness and restrictions and resentments that are also harmful to health. To help you to hear your heart, in this chapter I will make a distinction between healthy and unhealthy compromise, explore the impact of a head-heart conflict and recommend two shifts in awareness that will enable you to listen to and live in accordance with what your heart knows is best.

CORROSIVE HEAD–HEART COMPROMISES

Unhealthy compromise happens when you know that something isn't right for you, but you continue being, doing or having it anyway. Over time, having a conflicted head-heart compromise like this becomes corrosive because it is stressful for the body to constantly suppress your inner knowings, energetic impulses and intuitive desires. Compromise makes you fight against the creative forces of life that need to flow free for your health to greatly improve and your life purpose to be achieved.

Corrosive compromise buys into the illusion that you cannot have what your heart truly wants.

Compromise creates an inner conflict between what your heart knows is right and what your head believes is realistic. Living from your head, you end up governed by your beliefs and more inclined to base your future upon your past. If you have self-limiting beliefs your head will tell you that what you want isn't possible, for a range of reasons: you haven't had it before, you might end up in a worse position than at present, or you're not deserving of it yet. Your head will often convince you that it's safer to stay where you are than venture into the unknown. In doing so, you get talked out of going for what your heart truly wants and don't live fully and completely. Ultimately this convinces you to settle for a life that has become stale and stagnant instead of a taking the apparently risky route to remarkably better possibilities.

Having a head-heart conflict is tiring and stressful, whereas having head-heart harmony makes you healthier and happier.

My friend once described this compromised attitude to life as 'better burnt toast than no toast at all'. I love this phrase because it communicates corrosive compromise in beautifully simple terms, in which we accept 'less than' because we might end up without the thing we don't even really want in the first place! Read that again. We don't even want it, but don't let it go in case we end up without it. Totally bizarre when you think about it in these terms, but it is what's happening whenever we are compromising.

Common examples include:

- You stay in an unhappy relationship because you are afraid you might not meet anyone better.

- You stay in a job that you hate because you might not be able to get the job or create the business you want.

- You stay stuck living somewhere that you don't enjoy despite the deep desire to experience somewhere new.

Get your head out of the sand

One core thing to recognize about corrosive compromise is that no end of intellectual convincing can ever prevail over the immediate knowing of your heart. Consequently, it doesn't matter how much you try to convince yourself to the contrary of what your inner knowing is telling you, your heart can never be fooled.

The nagging feelings, the reflections from your universe and invitations to make a positive change will continue.

> *Burry your head in the sand if you want, but the sense that something isn't quite right will stick around.*

Not only that, but you will also often find your world will regularly reflect back any compromises in a myriad of ways. If you're in a job you hate, you will most likely meet people who tell you they love what they do. Or if you're in the wrong relationship you will either find a pile of wedding invitations on your doorstep or a stream of happy couples filling your Facebook newsfeed. Even choosing to read this book, from all the millions of books available, is an example of your world mirroring back to you what you need to know. There's no getting away from it and the longer your deny it, the more your body can end up suffering.

TOP TIP: SOME COMPROMISES ARE HELPFUL

Possessing a total unwillingness to compromise can make you stubborn and selfish, which again is stressful. In life, there are some kinds of compromise that are very helpful indeed. Healthy compromises offer the opportunity for you to surrender stubbornness, selfishness and static ideas, opening you up to unexpected yet enlivening experiences.

For example, I now love vegetarian sushi due to a helpful compromise. My friend Kyle Gray had a craving for it and I decided to use it as an opportunity to try something new that I'd always assumed I wouldn't like. Relationships are also an excellent training ground to practise healthy compromise. You won't always agree or want to do the same things, but due to the love you have for the other person, you make compromises to help their happiness and aid the harmony within the relationship. The trick is to know the difference between healthy and unhealthy compromise. With the general guidelines being: if there is harmony within your heart, mind, body and soul, then your compromise is clean.

WHAT IS YOUR HEART TELLING YOU?

I want to share two shifts in awareness that I've found essential for hearing the heart and being willing to act upon its innate wisdom – although it comes with a forewarning. We are about to venture into territory that can be dismissed by mainstream thinking. The following understandings have been known for centuries and taught by many spiritual teachers. However, due to the dependence in Western cultures on demanding physical proof along with the gradual rejection of anything that appears religious, these meta-physical perspectives have become somewhat unfashionable and therefore rejected by the mainstream. If you are willing to remain open-minded and open-hearted, then your quickest path to perfect health will reveal itself.

AWARENESS 1: I AM HERE FOR A SOUL PURPOSE

Knowing you are here for a soul purpose improves your relationship with life, gives your human experiences deeper meaning and encourages the courage that is often required to accomplish what you came here to do. I've intentionally used the word 'soul' instead of 'sole'. Mainly because your purpose is multi-faceted, including a range of 'tasks' within one ultimate soul purpose.

> *Ultimately, you are here to 'wake up' and know your Self as a complete being within unified consciousness.*

The more humanity moves from the heart to the head and away from oneness towards separateness, the more conflicted and disease-ridden we become. By knowing your unified Self, you find harmony within your heart and, in turn, with all other sentient beings and life itself. You experience your essence as eternal and this life as merely a blink of the cosmic eye. You wake up to the beauty of being, embrace all that human life has to offer and live courageously with grace, gratitude and liberty. Within this grander context, I believe we are also here to embody the virtues required to heal our negative traits that are born out of the ignorance of our real Self and perpetuated by the ego-based antics of the mind. To do this, you will be required to step through certain fears, live beyond self-imposed limits and ultimately realize the humbling magnitude of your oneness with divinity.

Physical conditions can occur to encourage you to stop and take stock of the messages you are ignoring. At the physical level, being in conflict with life can cause disease. Whereas at the meta-physical soul level, conditions can be gifts to help you fulfil the purpose for which you were born: living fully and completely. Learning to trust your heart is therefore vital. Given the chance, your heart will move you swiftly towards healing and true fulfilment. Thus making the inner journey from problems to perfection, stress to serenity and separation to oneness.

AWARENESS 2: I AM GIVEN EVERYTHING I NEED TO WAKE UP

You are here to know and be your Self fully in this body and world. Your soul task is to wake up from the illusionary conflicts of the individualistic mind. To accomplish this, you are placed in the most ideal environments and presented with the perfect people and circumstances that will give you the best opportunities to heal conflict and wake up to oneness. Despite the reality of everything happening to help you on your soul quest, I appreciate you might not always see it this way – in large because our life lessons are usually delivered through people, events and environments that we tend to judge as difficult, daunting and undesirable.

*Find peace with the people you find difficult
and the situations you find daunting.*

Wake-up calls

Just because things aren't always nice or easy, they are nonetheless necessary and evolutionary. In the same way that you can require an alarm to wake from a deep sleep – whereby the alarm needs to be contrasting enough with the silence to cause you to stir from the sleeping state – waking up spiritually is similar. Few people wake up during a comfortable life when everything is going to their plan. Instead, we often require wake-up calls that are suitably contrasting with the still, silent peaceful presence of our real Self to stir us from sleepwalking through life. Self-awakening usually requires you to step into the unknown by being things you've never been, knowing things you've never known and doing things you've never done. Due to the human trait of feeling safer with the familiar, many resist the openings they are given to rise above conditioning and venture into more evolutionary awakened ways of living.

One of my biggest wake-up calls happened a few years ago when, overnight, I went from having everything I thought I wanted to seeming to lose it all. I broke up with my girlfriend, lost contact with a child we'd been raising because the little girl wasn't biologically 'mine', felt forced to move out of the fancy house we'd been living in and was faced with major instability in my career as I had been running it with my now ex-partner. Yet, despite it being such a difficult time in my life, a business was also the catalyst I needed to go away for several months to meditate. Looking back, without the split, I wouldn't have been motivated to meditate and I wouldn't be enjoying the life I have today. This book and my previous four may not have existed and I wouldn't have been able to help so many people to benefit from meditation without that rock bottom wake-up call.

TOP TIP: HINDSIGHT HELPS

Apply what I'm saying to your own life. Consider some of your most difficult and daunting experiences in your life. Now consider what they taught you and helped you to achieve in the longer term. With the passage of time and access to newfound wisdom, you can see the perfection of even the most challenging of times. You can discover that by not getting what you thought you wanted; you were given exactly what you needed. By exploring this fully, hindsight can help you to clear conflict and be more open to life taking unexpected turns.

From selfish to self-less

Through your journey of waking up, you will notice a shift in your motives, too. If you are living from the mind, life will tend to be self-centred and there can be a high degree of selfishness involved. This is largely down to being unaware of the inner presence of peace, love and joy and needing to control life so you can get it from external sources. Unaware of the perfection within, you can end up living in states of fear and separation that can drive you to ruthlessly do whatever it takes to improve things and feel better. With force and without care or concern about the impact on others or the planet, you can single-mindedly pursue materialistic purposes linked to external success and the accumulation of power, possessions and prestige.

Selfishness is replaced by selflessness as one awakens.

Waking up, your motives naturally evolve. By engaging less in the mind-based concerns and conditioning and recognizing that we are all one within consciousness, your focus and actions come from an inner space of love and service. You become passionate about how you can bring peace, prosperity and positivity to the lives of others and the planet as a whole. I've seen this phenomenon within the people who use Mind Calm and Body Calm – once they enjoy the benefits for themselves they naturally want to become CALM coaches to share it with others. I believe this desire to 'pay it forward' is one of the most beautiful by-products that come from having a heard heart.

> *'What can I get?' changes to 'What can*
> *I give and how can I be of service?'*

Harmony and the return to health

Move away from destructive attitudes and behaviours that stem from a belief in separation and head-centred living. Remember, the head is concerned most about matters of survival and tends to live from a place of trepidation, limitation and doubt. Again, due to the terrain of the mind, with past disappointments, present insecurities and future fears, living from the head tends to also be tentative and lead to playing it safe. Through habitual judgements, resistances and attachments, you end up caught in a stressful relationship with situations, often reacting with anger, sadness, guilt and grief, all of which are signs of a lack of harmony within your heart.

Although physical problems can appear unfair and be uncomfortable, they can also be highly beneficial, if used as a guide to heal and evolve. It is wise to use your physical conditions to examine your attitudes towards yourself, others and life. See what makes you sad or angry or stressed, for example, and explore what you need to let go of and embody to live with more calm, compassion and contentment. Embrace what you may have previously perceived to be a problem because, as you now know, they are quickest route to the realization of your soul purpose. By learning to listen to your unheard heart, you become better placed to be in a state of harmony. When combined with the Body Calm meditation techniques and Embodying Exercise (which I will share in Chapter 14), you can help your body heal and stay healthy.

QUICK-START CURE: COMPROMISING QUESTION

To help you to listen to your heart and highlight any corrosive compromise that may be going on in your life, I invite you to be heroic by asking yourself this question:

Where in my life am I compromising?

Asking yourself this question has the power to bring into your awareness any area(s) of your life where you are currently in conflict with your heart. You will notice that this is not a question that requires much thinking. Quite the opposite in fact! You will find that if there is any compromise(s) in your life, the answer will come to you instantly. This is because it is your heart that is giving you the answer, not your mind. Your heart has known this and is delighted to be given the opportunity to be heard.

Irrespective of what came to mind, I urge you not to let this question be an opportunity to beat yourself up or feel forced to make any immediate changes. I say this in part because I don't want any hate mail from disgruntled ex-partners or bosses! But also because it is important for you to not put yourself under any additional pressure that could cause stress for your body. If a change is required it will happen at the perfect time and in the most loving and gentle way for all parties involved. If it feels right to make the change right now, then go for it. If it doesn't, then so be it. Be easy on yourself and continue along your journey with an increased awareness of any areas of your life that you need to be at peace with. The time to make the change will be presented and you will simply have to claim your heart desires. Stay vigilant to opportunities for making improvements that will support the fulfilment of your soul purpose. You owe it to yourself and everyone benefits if you follow your heart and are happy.

SUMMARY: UNHEARD HEART

- Listening to your heart is a heroic act because it requires you to trust your inner knowing over your mind-based logic or fears.

- Healthy compromise invites you to surrender your fixed opinions and preferences and be open to new and unexpected events and experiences.

- Unhealthy compromise happens when you continue to be, to do or to have things that no longer serve you, which your heart knows are not right for you.

- Unhealthy compromise buys into the illusion that you cannot have what you ultimately want.

- Continuing unhealthy compromise makes no sense, when you realize you don't want the thing you are resistant to losing and are attached to.

- Cleanse your life of corrosive compromise to create harmony within your heart, mind, body and soul and life.

- The two shifts in awareness that you need to live by and hear your heart are:

  - » I am here for a soul purpose

  - » I am given everything I need to wake up

- Look at your life and listen to your heart to find out what your unhealthy compromises are and be willing to evolve beyond your mind-based fears to embrace your awakened Self.

SELF-HEALING STATEMENTS: UNHEARD HEART

I am willing to hear my heart over my head.

I am free from the fear of the unknown.

I am excited to let go and let newness in.

I am here for a sacred soul purpose.

I am given what I need to wake up.

I am in harmony with my heart, mind, body, soul and life.

Chapter 13

UNAWAKE BEING

Through my explorations into how meditation can help us to enjoy deeper rest by reducing the time spent in states of stress, I've come to conclude that the solution ultimately boils down to a simple choice – a choice that will become both obvious and compelling by the time you've embodied what I'm going to share now. Within the context of bringing Part II to a consciously complete conclusion, this chapter summarizes some of what we've already explored and sets you up perfectly for getting the best from the Embodying Exercise coming next.

Due to the fact that your physicality experiences whatever you are perceiving, thinking about and aware of the most, learning to be aware of the aspects of life that bring wellness is evidently paramount. In my previous book, *Mind Calm*, I provided guidance on this all-important shift in awareness when I introduced the Content-Context Model, suggesting that there are two aspects of life that you can be aware of:

- the *content* of your life, and
- the *context* of your life.

For Body Calm, I've adapted the Content-Context Model to work within the setting of self-healing, physical performance and enhanced wellbeing. If you haven't read *Mind Calm*, (yet!), then rest assured that I will summarize the salient points that are relevant to Body Calm. It is also my hope that by offering a body-relevant version of the model here, those already familiar with the model will gain further insight into its power. As we progress through the Content-Context Model, you will also understand why I refer to the final secret source of stress as an 'Unawake Being'. You will see that if you live on the content side of the life, you inevitably end up with a limited, stress-filled and largely un-enjoyable life that is caused by being asleep to reality and your real Self. Whereas, if you hang out more on the context side, not only does your body benefit, but you get to wake up to the boundless brilliance and beauty of your being.

BODY CALM CONTENT-CONTEXT MODEL

With this model you will see in clear and simple terms the massive benefits gained from actively engaging GAAWO to live wide-awake. Let's start by applying it to your current moment so it's relevant to you. As you read this, within the area you are currently located, there might be furniture and flowers, your telephone or other belongings. These objects and any other things make up the *stuff* that you are presently aware of. What we tend to take for granted is that for all the stuff to exist, there needs to be the context of *space*. In fact, there has to be more space that stuff, otherwise the stuff wouldn't fit within the space. And although the stuff will eventually go, the space in which it inhabits is constant, ever-present and unchanging.

Content	Context
Stuff	Space

Exploring the content-context further, there will also be *sounds* happening within your environment that you can also be aware of. These noises may include a clock ticking, bird song, and the hum of traffic, music playing or people talking nearby. The interesting thing about sound is that it all happens within the context of *silence*. Without the silence, there would be no way of distinguishing the sound, because the silence is continuous and the sounds that are happening within it are only ever temporary.

Content	Context
Stuff	Space
Sounds	Silence

Moreover, the content of your current experience also includes *movement*: the movement of your eyes as they look around and eyelids when blinking; the movement of your fingers as you progress through the pages of this book; and the inward and outward movement of your chest as you breathe. Beyond your body, there will also be movement within your locale, whether it be cars driving past your window or the breeze making the trees sway nearby. All this movement happens within the context of *stillness*, which remains unmoved by the moving content happening within it.

Content	Context
Stuff	Space
Sounds	Silence
Movement	Stillness

To recap, we discovered something incredibly simple, yet, truly enlightening, once taken on board and embodied. The content of your life is made up of stuff, sound and movement and it all happens within the context of still, silent space. On top of that, the content is constantly changing and temporary whereas the context remains unchanged and permanent. So what's the big deal? Why would you want to be aware of the context? In a nutshell, your body feels, experiences and responds to whatever you are aware of. Therefore, by learning how to be attentive to the still, silent spacious context, your body experiences the peace-filled harmony that is always present.

The context of life is always in complete harmony.
Being aware of it means you can be too!

Now I've had the opportunity to share the Content-Context Model to thousands of people at my public talks, courses and retreats. Almost all of them have been unintentionally oblivious to the on-going presence of peace that is permanently present within and around them. Focused on the content of their mind, body and life, due to not being taught or encouraged to be aware of anything else, it's often a big, light-bulb moment when they realize there's more to life. I'm delighted to share there is much more to life, infinitely more, and by being context-aware, you can experience it for yourself.

BE CONTEXT AWARE TO BE CONSCIOUSLY AWARE

Continuing our exploration of the Content-Context Model, let's see how some of what we've shared within the previous secret sources of stress sits within this model, before investigating the wider implications. My on-going invitation to you is to go beyond the mind by being consciously aware. With this in mind, on which side of the model do you think the mind resides? You know you have a mind because you are aware of it. As a result, the mind is the content and the conscious awareness is the context. Quite wonderfully, when you become consciously aware, you automatically connect with the calming, still, silent spaciousness because consciousness is inherently still, silent and spacious.

The eye of awareness is still, silent and spacious.

Also, you may remember I previously asked the question: *How do you know you have a body?* The answer was you know you have a body because you are aware of it. Linking this with the Content-Context model, this means that your physical form sits on the content side whereas the non-physical aspects of you remain on the right i.e. the context. The implications of this are immense.

Content	Context
Stuff	Space
Sounds	Silence
Movement	Stillness
Mind	Conscious awareness
Physical	Non-physical
Pain/Suffering	Pain-free/Serenity

Let's say you have a physical condition occurring within your body. It means there is always a non-physical aspect of you that is whole and completely still and silent. By being aware of non-physical consciousness, you can experience the peace and perfection of the Self that exists beyond the body. As a result, you need not suffer even if your body is uncomfortable or unhealthy, as long as you are aware of the context. As most suffering comes from thinking about problems, when you stop thinking about the physical condition, suffering naturally diminishes. Furthermore, because you feel what you focus on, again, focusing on the calm context, your experience is automatically more peaceful. Wow!

I THINK AND I AM

Leading on from this, due to thinking happening in your mind, it means the context of who you think you are, is the 'I AM'. Living from the mind, you end up relating and reacting to life based upon your self-image and conditioned personality. Or said slightly differently, you project out and need to protect the ideas about who you think you are or should be. However, when you interact with life from context-awareness, you are then no longer governed or limited by the personality you believe yourself to be. The 'I AM' aspect of you is permanent and beyond temporary personality traits. You will find that the best way to be will flow through you and your body will no longer need to endure the pressure and stress associated with trying to live up to an idea of who you think you should be. To explore this more deeply, use the Booster Calm Thought on page 157.

Content	Context
Stuff	Space
Sounds	Silence
Movement	Stillness
Mind	Conscious awareness
Physical	Non-physical
Pain/Suffering	Pain-free/Serenity
I Think	I Am

BEYOND BELIEFS BY BEING YOUR TRUE SELF

The content of your thinking is determined largely by your beliefs. When on the content side, you end up perceiving a distorted version of life via your collection of beliefs that are only ever relatively true, this is because while you may believe something, someone else may believe the complete opposite. Who's right? The answer is rather confusingly, both and neither. Although the beliefs appear to be true as far as both parties are concerned, they are only a relative rightness. For example, one person may believe that it's natural to gain weight the older they get, while the other believes they will stay slim for the duration of their days. In both cases, their beliefs are likely to be proven right. However, the reality is, neither of the opposing beliefs is ultimately true. Truth on the other hand is absolute. It is true for every person everywhere, which is the main difference between beliefs and truths. As long as you stay focused on the content side, you will remain unfamiliar with the truth of your Self and the true nature of reality.

Due to beliefs being relatively true, it is natural to meet people and experience circumstances that are contrary to what you believe. Remaining fixed in your belief system, you inevitably end up in conflict. As you know, conflict causes stress and other physiological states that are harmful to health. However, on the plus side, if you are willing to step beyond your beliefs by being aware of the context, then you will find far less conflict occurs. You discover that because truth is absolute, there is no opposition to be in conflict with and harmony is the natural by-product of being contextually aware.

Content	Context
Stuff	Space
Sounds	Silence
Movement	Stillness
Mind	Conscious awareness
Physical	Non-physical
Pain/Suffering	Pain-free/Serenity
I Think	I Am
Beliefs	Truth
Judgement	Love
Resistance	Allowance
☹ Emotions	☺ Emotions

Context-awareness also feels great! When you go beyond beliefs, you don't have to juggle the countless judgements created by the mind. Without judgement, there is no reason to resist and through your inner harmony with what was, is and might be, life leads to many more higher level emotional experiences such as happiness, compassion and peace. Joyous without judgements there are also no reasons not to love yourself, other people and life. You experience the perfection of life; you get to experience true love, which is unconditional.

HARMONY AND HEALING

I hope by now that you are seeing very clearly that living aware of the context side of life is a wonderful place to hang out. Remarkably, the plus points and beneficial by-products don't end here. In relation to physical healing, there are also a number of healthy paybacks from paying attention to the still silent side of things. Caught up in the content, the body is more inclined to exist within the fight/flight/freeze stressful states that breeds *dis*-ease. As your body follows and feels the sometimes-frantic fantasies of the mind, stress hormones are regularly released and the body engages its survival responses. However, when you become conscious of and rest within the still, silent presence of being, you spontaneously create harmony.

Harmony allows healing and health to flourish.

Remember, the body is able to handle short bouts of stress; it's the long-term on-going tension that takes its toll and makes it more prone to problems. Even if you do face situations that are potentially dangerous, difficult or daunting, by engaging GAAWO and using the Body Calm meditation technique, your body will be less affected. Ultimately, still, silence space is absolute and has no opposite to become unbalanced by. So being context-aware, you will find you hang out more often in harmony with a body in-balance.

POOR TO PEAK PERFORMANCE

Better still, you will also find that your balanced body becomes more able to perform at its best in a vast array of social, sporting and business environments. One of the main reasons I believe people don't get the performance they want from their body during sporting activities, social events or in work, whether it be manual or office based, is because they lack context awareness. Take a moment to imagine. It's the final of the Football World Cup and the teams are so equally matched that after the 90 minutes and extra time, it's come down to penalties. The coach calls your name and the referee hands you the ball at the halfway line. You then take the long walk to the penalty spot where after what feels like an eternity you place the ball down on the grass. You take a few steps back and prepare to take the shot.

What happens next is partly down to skill and mostly down to the mind and body being able to do what they've done a million times on the practice pitch – hit the back of the net. But if you're in your mind, thinking can distract you. Having picked up a few limiting beliefs many years before that pivotal moment, thoughts of doubt jump to the forefront of your focus, quickly followed by nervousness and fear that floods your body, causing it to become more tense and tentative.

Now contrast this with what would happen, if you were to hang out on the context-side. Consciously aware, you are fully present in the here and now, within your head is silence and in your muscles is the potent power of presence. Your breathing is relaxed, your body balanced. Free from thinking; you feel the confidence that comes from being beyond the judgements and insecurities of the mind. Feeling secure and fully surrendered to whatever happens next, you step forward with a congruent and courageous heart, mind, body and soul.

I appreciate this is a rather extreme example. I use it to stress the importance of stillness when it comes to getting the best from your body. The same principles apply for if you are in the business context with a tight deadline, a big presentation or important interview. Being context-aware gives you greater clarity, better decision making, enables you to access your knowledge and skills and even provides the ability to be a powerful presence in times it's required.

Content	Context
Poor performance	Peak performance

Whether you are busy at your desk or active on the field, track or yoga mat, being still by being beyond your busy mind is of great benefit. I'd say it is the difference between average and amazing, so I urge you to work and play with it by remaining attentive to stillness.

> *Being still doesn't mean you stop moving. It simply means being aware of the inner presence of stillness as you actively move and perform.*

MELT WITHIN THE IMMORTAL

Earlier in the book I said the 'body is the temporary home for eternal consciousness'. The more you spend time on the context side of life, the more you can discover that the consciousness you are experiencing is timeless and has no beginning or end. Infinite with no outer boundaries, edges or end points, still silent space is permanent and exists beyond the temporary body. As you allow your ideas of what you think you are to melt within the immortal presence of Who You Really Are, you discover there is life after death because ultimately there is no death in the realms you now know. There's also no birth. Eternally existing, there is a unified consciousness looking through the eyes of a temporary physical temple for the purpose of experiencing itself through itself – fully.

Experiencing the truth of Who You Really Are, there is no fear about the demise or death of the physical form. On the contrary, there is awe and wonder for all the great gifts this human life gives. Your relationship with life is transformed and oneness with divinity becomes your awakened way of being your Self while living completely.

Content	Context
Stuff	Space
Sounds	Silence
Movement	Stillness
Mind	Conscious awareness
Physical	Non-physical
I Think	I Am
Beliefs	Truth
Judgement	Love
Resistance	Allowance
☹ Emotions	☺ Emotions
Fight/Flight/Freeze	Harmony/Healing
Stress state	Self-healing state
Imbalance	In-balance
Poor performance	Peek performance
Temporary	Permanent
Mortal	Immortal
BUSY MIND + BODY	MIND + BODY CALM

QUICK-START CURE: CONTEXT AWARENESS

This quick-start cure helps you to become aware of the context. To get the best results, adhere to the same golden rules as GAAWO: Play with it, don't think about it and do it now:

1. Maintain a gaze ahead at the book.

2. Notice your left shoulder (without looking at it).

3. Notice your right foot (without looking at it).

4. Notice the space between you and the book. (Don't try to see it because it's invisible. Just notice the space.)

5. Notice the space around the book. (Again, don't try to see it because it is invisible.)

6. Notice the space in the entire room. (You won't see the space, but you will be able to sense and feel it.)

As you notice the space in the entire room, what word(s) best describe your inner experience as you continue to be context aware? Answers usually include calm, still, quiet, home, expansive and so on. In the end, you need do so little to receive so much. Simply by being aware of the context, you can create harmony within your heart, body, mind and soul that can help to bring about brilliant health.

SUMMARY: UNAWAKE BEING

- To enjoy deeper rest and less stress, be context aware.

- The content of life is made up of stuff, sound and movement.

- The context of life consists of still, silent spaciousness.

- Your mind is part of the content, whereas your conscious awareness is the context of every though, feeling, action and circumstance in your life.

- The context of the body is non-physical presence.

- Pain and suffering occurs within the content, however that which is aware is pain-free and serene.

- The 'I AM' is permanent and beyond personality traits.

- Beliefs are relatively true and exist on the content side of life. Truth is absolute and the context of all beliefs.

- Context awareness moves you into a state of love as it is beyond judgement, resistance and attachment.

- The body is more inclined to live in a state of fight/flight/ freeze when you focus on the content.

- Beyond the limitations of the mind, you perform much more effectively when context aware.

- Fear of death can dissolve the more you get to know the immortal aspect of your contextual Self.

- When you are aware of the context, you allow harmony to exist in your heart, mind, body and soul.

- Meditation is a proven technique for moving your awareness from the content to the context.

SELF-HEALING STATEMENTS: UNAWAKE BEING

I am the still silent spacious Self.

I am the non-physical context of my physical body.

I am beyond pain and suffering when context aware.

I am that I am and not what I think.

I am the truth that is the context of all beliefs.

I am beyond conflict when aware of the context.

I am beyond mental interference and able to perform.

I am eternal and immortal with nothing to fear.

I am the context of unconditional love.

SUMMARY: THE SEVEN SECRET SOURCES OF STRESS

These sources of stress are the different ways that you can unintentionally create inner conflict. By clearing the conflict, harmony is restored and health and happiness become your natural states to be in.

1. Uncomfortable emotions

Emotions are energy that needs to move freely to fulfil their positive purposes. Suppressing emotions creates energy blockages and limits your body's ability to heal. Recognizing you are not your emotions, peace is not the absence of emotions and the more emotions the better is key to healing. Befriend your feelings by learning how to be comfortable feeling uncomfortable.

2. Unhealthy beliefs

Although stress is known as a major cause of bad health, conflict is the hidden cause of harmful forms of stress. Your beliefs determine how you react to life including what you allow and resist. Unhealthy beliefs are any that justify resistance and attachment. To increase health you must go beyond your beliefs by being open to all possible human experiences.

3. Unforgiven past

When a person experiences an undesirable significant emotional event, the energy associated with it can become stuck and also cause the body to be in a perpetual state of stress, as though the event is still happening. By forgiving the past, the blocked energy can move freely again, the stress response disengages, and the event or experience is allowed to complete its positive purpose.

4. Unwanted present

Being in conflict with your current life circumstances causes chronic stress, bad health and unhappiness. Acknowledge your realms of resistance and areas of attachment and learn how to let life be enough, exactly as it is. Also, the ultimate cause of an unwanted present is *not* being present. Being consciously aware brings you back to the now and gives you peace with the present moment and freedom from problems.

5. Unloved body

Fighting your physical form is harmful to your health. To befriend your body it helps to know your body is not working against you but instead adapting to survive. Once this is appreciated, you can explore the reasons for why your body would feel the need to adapt, and then make positive changes to encourage it to adapt again and return to a more preferred state of health. It is also fundamental to recognize that although you have a body, you are not your body. Knowing this enables you to calmly coexist with any condition and help healing.

6. Unheard heart

Ignoring the messages from your heart can lead to a compromised life that is stressful due to the conflict between your mind and soul. Appreciating that you are here for a soul purpose and given what you need to wake up, you learn to listen and live in agreement with your heart, and harmony is gained within you mind, body and soul to allow for greater health and happiness.

7. Unawake being

Make the inner shift from content to context i.e. stuff, sound and movement to the still, silent spaciousness. By moving your attention to the context, you become aware of the inner, still, silent presence of calm conscious awareness, you love and allow more, activate a more harmonious healing state, live in-balance and allow the body to heal more easily and function optimally.

Part III

EMBODYING CALM

Chapter 14

EMBODYING EXERCISE

Embodying calm is central to the Body Calm approach. As you may remember, the CALM part of the name stands for 'Conscious Awareness Life Meditation', meaning that to Embody Calm is to be Self-aware and use the power of the mind–body connection and calm consciousness to encourage self-healing and sustained health. By doing so, you don't let your past or current conditions define who you are. Rather, by resting in the powerful presence of your real Self, you can be the person that life is inviting you to be. The Embodying Exercise can be used whenever you have a physical condition that needs healing or at times you encounter stressful situations in daily life. It clears conflict by helping you to be at peace with resistances and attachments through the embodiment of certain virtue(s) that cause life events and experiences to serve their purpose and become complete. Being the virtue(s) creates harmony within your heart, mind, body and soul, which is the foundation to health and happiness.

Embodying calm ultimately enables
you to live fully and completely.

Embodying is not a thinking-based exercise but one that only works if you engage it from conscious awareness and by feeling your way through it. This is down to the exercise being a bridge between your physical body and consciousness. The mind relies on effort and linear time and works within limits. It needs justification, evidence and for you to do things to eventually become better or more. Consciousness, on the other hand, is already complete and requires no doing on your part to be. It is *already* the virtues and by being consciously aware, you can quite literally download the virtues into your body and being – immediately, not after you've done years of therapy or engaged in lots of effort to try to become them, but now.

However, if you rely on your thinking mind to achieve this, it won't work because your intellect will usually require reasons to justify the eventual becoming of these positive traits. Your beliefs may stand in the way of your ability to simply embody and enliven them from a consciously aware perspective. If this is sounding too simplistic, confusing or impossible, then recognize that it's your mind saying so. If you are willing to let go of the thinking mind and follow the instructions, you may be pleasantly surprised by how quickly changes can occur.

Although it is one of the simplest exercises you may ever use, there are subtleties in the instructions that you need to be clear on to use it effectively. Once you understand it, you will be amazed that something so effortless can reap such massive rewards. I believe this is the future of content-free change work, where you don't need to talk or think at length about your problems. Instead, you simply need to be Self-aware and embody the positive traits that life is inviting you to step up and wake up into. So stay openhearted and use the exercise within the context of the following three distinctions.

1. AWARENESS + ATTENTION

Awareness is still, wide-ranging and all-inclusive. Attention on the other hand jumps from one thing to the next, tends to be scattered and takes effort to direct. Attention tends to become fixed upon certain events or experiences whereas awareness observes from a more benevolent, bigger-picture perspective. The difference can be subtle, so it is easier to experience it for yourself than try to understand intellectually. Right now, focus your attention on your body. Having done that, notice where your attention has gone. More often than not, it will have moved to specific parts of your body, most likely, the bits that caught your attention. These might be areas of discomfort or parts that are emotionally charged i.e. you like or dislike. In doing so, your focus will have become narrow and honed in on the specific parts of your body.

Now, be aware of your body by having a more general awareness of it. Feel the difference? Your experience will be wider, taking in all aspects of your physical form, from a consciously aware perspective. If this wasn't your experience, then you will have habitually started using your attention again, instead of resting in your wider awareness. A subtle difference, yes, but you must use the Embodying Exercise by being 'in-awareness' not 'in-attention' for it to work. Otherwise you will get caught up in the content of your mind instead of harnessing the power of the conscious context.

2. FEEL + FEELINGS

Embodying requires you to 'feel with your awareness'. When doing so, you will be able to experience emotional feelings and physical sensations while remaining aware. To appreciate the importance, answer this: *What emotions are you currently feeling? Or what physical sensations are going on in your body at present?* Now, engage GAAWO and notice the difference when you observe: *What is it like to feel the overall feeling of the emotions and/or physical sensations happening now?*

Feel the difference? The first two questions cause you to identify into and engage with individual feelings and physical sensations. Whereas when you feel with your awareness how your emotions/sensations feel, you do so in a more aware and all-encompassing manner. You focus less on the specific feelings and more on the overall united feeling. Although this may seem rather pedantic, it makes for a world of difference when using the exercise. Again, it will enable you to stay in the context awareness rather than lose your Self in the content.

3. EXPERIENCING + THINKING

Consciously experiencing is feeling with your awareness without any definitions, judgements or descriptions of what you are feeling. Read that again because it is fundamental. It is very easy to drop into the mind, due to thinking being a habit. But to embody, you need to experience with your awareness instead of think your way through the steps. This is because your mind is one step removed from the 'now experience'. So if you end up thinking about the exercise, it will become 'heady' and you won't embody the changes as deeply into your physical form as you can when you are present and aware.

Play with experiencing it now. Without attaching any definitions, judgements or descriptions, feel with your awareness the space you are currently occupying within the area you are reading this book. Experience it now. Feel with your awareness what the space is like. Don't think about it or engage in any mind-based commentary. Simply feel the space with your awareness. Now, try it with your body. Within your body there may be physical sensations and emotions happening. But without thinking about any of it, feel your body with your awareness without any definitions, judgements or descriptions. Just be gently alert with your awareness upon your entire body.

Following these instructions, you will notice that you are currently calmly coexisting with your body. Although there may still be sensations and emotions present, they are happening within the quiet and peaceful context of consciousness. You are feeling instead of getting lost in the specific feelings and sensations. If you can adhere to these distinctions and follow the instructions provided, you will be able to rest in the powerful presence of your aware Self and embody the virtues that life is inviting you to step up and wake up into being.

My mind–body mentor, Peter Blake, originally formulated a version of the Embodying Exercise and I've adapted it for Body Calm.

TOP TIP: LESS RELEASING, MORE EMBODYING

Perhaps surprisingly, with the Embodying Exercise you are not aiming to 'release' the conflict because wanting it gone is just another subtle form of resistance. Instead you are going to feel it fully with your awareness as you embody the virtue(s). Releasing things you don't want can cause energy to move outward whereas embodying allows energy to remain within you. The more energy you have, the better your health. For the record, I'm also not asking you to suffer when feeling the resistance or attachment. You will be able to calmly coexist with it if you feel with your awareness throughout the exercise.

EMBODYING EXERCISE (EE) INSTRUCTIONS

Decide what you want to help heal with the Embodying Exercise. This will usually be a physical, emotional or life issue you are dealing with. Then do the following:

1. Be context aware

Begin by engaging GAAWO, or if you prefer, be aware of the context of space in the room. Rest in awareness throughout the entire exercise. If you ever notice yourself thinking, analysing or trying to figure things out, then re-engage context awareness before continuing.

2. Feel with awareness

This step helps you to describe what the physical condition/ life situation feels like and then find an event or experience to do the Embodying Exercise on. If you are using the EE alongside the directories in Chapter 15, ignore the first question underneath and instead feel with your awareness the mind-based cause(s) from the list(s), then with the cause(s) that resonate with you, consider the second question below.

Remaining aware, feel with your awareness and ask:

- *What does this physical condition (or stressful life situation) feel like to experience?*

Use words that describe what the condition/situation feels like to experience. For example, pressure, irritated, restricted, weak, drained, trapped, separate, under attack, invaded, helpless, alone, vulnerable, etc. Note that these words are not labels that you've been given to call the condition. They are how the physical condition/life situation feels when experienced from awareness. When you have a descriptive word, ask:

- *Where has this feeling or experience shown up in my life?*

Remain aware and let a current or past event or experience reveal itself to you now.

3. Clear the conflict

Once you have found an event or experience that has been unresolved, continue to feel with your awareness while doing the following:

- Be aware of and feel for resistance within the event or experience.

- While continuing to feel the resistance, become aware of the attachment that is connected to this resistance and feel the attachment, too.

- Bring the resistance and attachment together to feel them as one experience.

- Feel for the outer edges of the resistance and attachment within one experience.

You do not need to intellectually know what you are resisting or attached to. It's OK too if it comes to mind. Just be careful not to get caught thinking about it. It will work as long as you fully experience the resistance and attachment by feeling it with awareness.

4. Embody the virtue

While still being willing to feel the resistance and attachment, in relation to the feeling or experience, ask:

- *What virtue is most appropriate for* this *experience?* Continue to feel the resistance and attachment and allow the virtue that life is inviting you to embody to reveal itself.

- Feel what the virtue feels like for a few moments before experiencing what you feel like *as* the virtue.

- Feel what the virtue feels like *without* attaching to anything. For example, unrelated to a person or an event.

• Be the virtue, letting it permeate you. This is what the embodiment of the virtue feels like.

Examples of virtues		
Acceptance	Love	Security
Courage	Faith	Forgiveness
Contentment	Understanding	Strength
Harmony	Certainty	Wholeness
Truth	Worthiness	Freedom
Compassion	Wisdom	Peace
Openness	Trust	Power
Service	Surrender	Goodness

Allow your own virtues to reveals themselves to you.

Having done the Embodying Exercise, you will feel different about the issue that you were finding stressful. The physical condition may also feel better or your relationship with it will feel more harmonious. If not, you may need to use it again on the same event, experience or emotions. Although this exercise may seem complicated or involve several steps, with practice you will find it works very quickly.

Meet Jessica, who had a headache

When speaking about what the condition felt like she described the headache as 'being under pressure'. When considering where the feeling or experience had been showing up in her life she said, 'it's how I feel around my mum.' The conflict came from resisting 'feeling forced to be a certain way' with an attachment to 'wanting to be loved and accepted as I am'. While feeling the resistance and attachment with her awareness, the most appropriate virtue that presented itself was 'self-acceptance'. Jessica then embodied the virtue and after a few moments, reported the headache had eased and within half an hour it had completely gone.

Meet Peter, who was feeling emotional and stressed

When describing the emotion he realized it was feelings of 'fear around the release of his first book'. Tuning into the resistance it became clear it was 'resisting being seen, criticized and failing' and the attachment was to him 'hiding in his comfort zone'. While feeling the resistance and attachment, the most appropriate virtue that presented itself was 'calming courage'. Having embodied it, he reported instantly feeling less scared and more confident and over the next hour these feelings increased. Peter wrote to me afterwards saying he 'went from feeling incredibly low to high and was amazed it could happen with such a simple exercise'.

If you have a problem of any kind then there will be inner conflict that the Embodying Exercise can help to resolve. The trick is to allow yourself to fully feel the resistance and attachment with your awareness. Remember, events happen to help you 'download' the positive virtues that will allow you to live more fully and completely. And by embodying the virtues you create inner harmony that helps healing and staying healthy.

TOP TIP: USE THIS AS YOU WOULD MEDICINE

When prescribed medicine from a doctor, you wouldn't take one pill and give up if you didn't feel immediate benefits. Similarly, to get the best from the Embodying Exercise, you may need do it a number of times, on a range of issues, over a prolonged period for you see the evidence of your positive work reflected within your body. Although the body can change quickly, it is highly recommended you have a similar mind-set towards it as you would towards medicine.

SUMMARY: EMBODYING EXERCISE

- *Be context aware* by engaging GAAWO or noticing the space you occupy.

- *Feel with awareness* and describe what the condition/life situation feels like to experience before considering where this feeling or experience has shown up in your life. When using EE alongside the directories in the next chapter, the lists of mind-based causes will give the description of how you feel, so you only need to find the life event or experience before moving on to step 3.

- *Clear the conflict* by feeling with your awareness the resistance and attachment together as one experience. This helps you to experience it fully and completely and collapse the conflict.

- *Embody the virtue* by letting the most appropriate virtue reveal itself and then feel what it is like to be it now. This helps you to heal your relationship with the potential mind-based causes of the physical condition and be more calm in relation to the stressful life situation.

Chapter 15

WHEN THE BODY SPEAKS

The physical body is a remarkably clever, conscious being. I believe it exists to allow you to have the life experiences you need to embody the virtues that will fulfil the purposes for which you were born. In many ways, the body is more conscious and aware than the thinking mind. Whereas the mind tends to create stress, separation and conflict, the body always wants oneness and harmony, and is constantly adapting to find balance. As a result, your body is a brilliant barometer as to how in harmony you are, offering ongoing, real-time feedback in relation to how aligned you are to the most aware and harmonious aspects of your Self.

There is much that can be learnt from the body for those who are willing and able to understand its many meaningful messages.

Often your body speaks to both your mind and soul in very symbolic ways, which are a perfect reflection of your relationship with life. When you can interpret the meaningful messages from your body, you're able to tell a massive amount about your mental, emotional and spiritual states. In this chapter you'll find five directories to help you find the possible mind-based cause(s) of your current conditions and guidance on how you can act upon its invitations to return to harmony. It is recommended that you use these directories alongside the Embodying Exercise to help healing:

Body Directory: Listing the common mind-based causes of conditions relating to the main parts of your body.

Organ Directory: Listing the common mind-based causes of conditions relating to the main organs of your body.

Systems Directory: Listing the common mind-based causes of conditions relating to the 12 body systems.

Senses Directory: Offering guidance on the common mind-based causes of issues relating to your five senses.

Conditions Directory: Listing the common mind-based causes relating to 101 physical conditions.

These directories have come about from my observations during many years of clinical practice and my investigations into how the body speaks to the mind and soul. In addition, I've also trained hundreds of practitioners in my methods from over 15 countries and so had the unique opportunity to read thousands of case studies submitted by students taking my academy courses. Combining all this data, I've been able to see a number of trends in the common mind-based causes of physical conditions. By sharing them with you here, I hope they help you to discover what your body may be saying through the conditions it has created. I always recommend you tune into your body and find your own causes when possible, using the complete Embodying Exercise.

What is your body saying via your physical conditions?

ABOUT THE DIRECTORIES

The body is an indicator for what is in and out of harmony within your mind, emotions and spiritual Self. As a natural consequence, we view physical conditions more as a red flag to draw our attention to where any disharmony is being highlighted. Highly symbolic, the body tends to present physical symptoms in the areas of your body that serve particular purposes, with these functions reflecting what's happening in your life. As a result, we are more interested in the functions of the body parts, organs, systems and senses and how the experience of the physical condition feels like to you. So instead of getting too caught up in the labels you've been given for any condition, you want to focus more on the function of the body areas where you have physical issues, how your condition feels and how this is being reflected in your life.

For example, the purpose of the liver is purification, so if you have a physical issue there, you want to explore areas of your life that feel toxic and/or overloaded with negativity. The small intestine performs the function of absorption. So if you have issues relating to that part of your body, you want to explore situations in your life that you are rejecting and/or in which you have not been able to absorb what's happening/happened fully.

For the first four directories, find the body part, organ, system or sense that has a physical condition happening within it. Then read through the common mind-based cause that people with issues relating to that aspect of their body tend to be dealing with. You will know you've found a possible cause because it will feel true to you – almost like I've just told you what's been going on in your life. Then once you've found the potential cause, ask: *Where has this feeling or experience shown up in my life?* You want to allow for a person, event or experience to come into your mind. Don't overthink it. If you remain in GAAWO, you will find the perfect thing will come to mind. Once it does, turn to the Embodying

Exercise (see pages 195–8) to clear the conflict and embody the virtue(s) you need in order to allow for more harmony in relation to the event or experience. Once you get to know how it works, you will find it very easy and natural to tune into the body, feel with your awareness what's in disharmony and do the Embodying Exercise to aid rest and recovery.

The body has created the condition to highlight something important to you. It can also uncreate the condition too, once the reason has been resolved.

To help your body to heal, you need to be willing to feel, experience and embody from a Self-aware perspective. Don't let it become a thinking-based process, otherwise you may remain one step removed from the physical and emotional experience, and it will be less effective. For some conditions, there may be multiple experiences that are in conflict and you will need to use the Embodying Exercise a few times on different things – or a few times on the same issue. Enjoy the exploration into the mind-body-soul connection. Use it as an opportunity to take steps towards fulfilling your purpose of living fully and completely.

EXTRA SUPPORT

GUIDED SELF-HEALING MEDITATIONS

I've recorded a series of guided meditations based upon these Body Calm Directories, and these can give you extra support to help heal the mind-based causes of specific conditions. Please visit www.sandynewbigging.com for track listings and to download them.

SUMMARY: HOW TO USE THE DIRECTORIES

- Decide upon the condition you want to help heal.

- Turn to the most relevant directory and read through the common mind-based causes.

- When you find one that resonates with you, let the life event or experience come to mind and from a consciously aware perspective, feel it fully.

- Use the Embodying Exercise to clear conflict and embody the virtues that will allow you to return to harmony, health and happiness.

BODY PART DIRECTORY

This lists the common mind-based causes of conditions relating to the main parts of the body.

BACKGROUND TO THE BODY PART DIRECTORY

Although you have a male or female body, everyone has masculine and feminine energy and elements within them. The Body Part Directory takes account of the long-known phenomenon that the different sides of the body link with different sexes. I've observed that if the masculine-feminine energetic equilibrium becomes imbalanced, it will show up in how you relate to life and the body can reflect how you feel through physical symptoms. Again, the loss of balance stems from inner conflict and not yet embodying the positive virtues that allow you to maintain a harmonious balance.

Using Chinese Medicine to help diagnosis

Traditional Chinese Medicine (TCM) is an ancient system of medicine that uses a range of methods for diagnosing and treating the physical form. Although it is believed to be 2,000 years old, it is very relevant today for discovering the possible mind-based causes for what's happening within your body. The Body Part

Directory draws on the TCM understandings about the different sides of the body relating to either masculine or feminine. Within the context of the model masculine is not 'male' and feminine is not 'female' so, to use this model effectively, it is best not to try to fit them into the classical concepts about male and female traits. Using them to help diagnosis is more about determining whether your masculine and feminine qualities are in balance, or not. Here's a quick overview of the qualities associated with the left and right sides of the body:

Masculine side

The right side of the body is linked with the masculine aspects. It corresponds with giving, moving, manifesting and doing. It is how you create in the external world and is associated primarily with the outflow of energy. If there is an imbalance, you will hold back from giving, be unassertive, doubtful, lack confidence and not be doing what is required to create.

Feminine side

The left side of the body is linked with the feminine aspects. As a general rule, the feminine side is about receiving, being and the inner self. It is how you receive and is associated primarily with the inflow of energy. If there is an imbalance, there will usually be unrest within your inner sense of self and you will be closed off to allowing in certain aspects of your external life.

> *When in harmony you will have balance within the masculine and feminine, giving and receiving and being and doing sides of yourself.*

HOW TO USE THE BODY PART DIRECTORY

For the Body Part Directory, you will see the common mind-based causes are listed under the left and right sides of the body. So if you have a physical problem, which predominantly sits on one side of your body, you will find this directory especially useful. Also, if your issue is happening on both sides (or in the middle) of your body, then you'll want to explore both the masculine and feminine aspects. You will find it will shed light on why problems have shown up in specific areas of your body. To use the directory:

1. **Locate the side(s) of the body:** Notice if your problem is mainly on one side of your body or recall if it started on one side of your body. If it is on both, take account of both masculine and feminine aspects in relation to the mind-based causes.

2. **Link the body part with the mind-based cause:** Scan down the directory (see pages 209–215) to find the body part and then read the common causes of issues happening within that body part. When reading, be context-aware and notice if you resonate with any of the common cause(s).

3. **Find the specific life event/experience:** Once you've found the potential mind-based cause, ask: *Where is this experience showing up in my life?* Engage GAAWO and let the person, event or situation come to mind. If you cannot think of anything, don't overthink it. It will work as long as you experience how the mind-based cause feels.

4. **Use the Embodying Exercise to help heal:** Use steps 3 + 4 of the Embodying Exercise on pages 195–8 to clear the conflict and embody the virtue(s) you need that will bring harmony to the event or experience that may be causing your disharmony and physical condition.

For example, if you have neck pain on your left side. Ask: *What viewpoints of my inner knowing am I resisting or where in my life am I attached to my inner voice saying something else?* With GAAWO engaged, once you have recalled the event or experience, use the Embodying Exercise (picking up the exercise at step 3 because the directory will have already helped you do steps 1 and 2). Having embodied the virtue, you may find that the body part feels more at ease and you can make any positive changes that your body has been inviting you to do.

PLEASE NOTE: FOR GUIDE PURPOSES ONLY

Aim to allow your own mind-based causes to be revealed to you by considering the body-part function in relation to your life (see steps 1 + 2 of the Embodying Exercise). For example, hands relate to grasping, so where are you grasping and/or holding on in your life? If the physical problem is occurring on both side of the body, use the Embodying Exercise steps 3 + 4 on both masculine and feminine mind-based causes that resonate with you.

Body parts + Causes	
Face	
Function	Expression
Left side	Resistance to facing aspects of your inner self that you perceive as ugly/bad +/or hiding your inner feelings/knowings +/or attached to seeing yourself in a particular way.
Right side	Resistance to facing the world +/or unwilling/unable to express and give fully when doing + creating +/or attached to being publically seen in a positive way that is loved/accepted/respected.
Neck	
Function	Viewpoints
Left side	Resistance to accepting certain viewpoints of your inner knowing +/or attachment to your inner voice saying something else.

(continued)

Body parts + Causes	
Neck (continued)	
Right side	Attached to giving your viewpoints in relation to what you do +/or resistance to listening + acting upon externally received viewpoints.
Shoulders	
Function	Lifting (+ carrying)
Left side	Resistance to allowing yourself to be lifted up/ carried +/or resistance to picking up or carrying new ways of being within your inner self.
Right side	Resistance to picking up/carrying part(s) of your external world +/or resistance to picking up/carrying different ways of doing + creating.
Chest	
Function	Expansion
Left side	Restricted by what you are receiving, feeling limited in how or who you can be +/or feeling constricted within your inner sense of self.
Right side	Restricted by what you have to give, how you can give +/or limited in what you can do +/or constricted by external life circumstance(s).
Ribs	
Function	Protection (+ life force)
Left side	Feeling vulnerable in relation to what you are receiving +/or lacking inner life force +/or attached to finding sanctuary within your inner self.
Right side	Unable to give protection to others +/or lacking flow in external life +/or vulnerable/under attack from your external world
Upper back	
Function	Carrying
Left side	Resistance to allowing yourself to be carried +/or feeling a burden/heaviness within your inner self.

Body parts + Causes	
Right side	Resistance to carrying a person, event or thing +/or feeling external life/world too heavy to carry.
Middle back	
Function	Connection
Left side	Blocked to receiving connection +/or disconnected from certain aspects of your inner Self.
Right side	Holding back from giving connection +/or disconnected from aspects of external life/world.
Lower back	
Function	Support
Left side	Resistance to being your own support +/or attached to using the thinking mind for support instead of being supported by your soul-self.
Right side	Resistance to giving support +/or feeling unsupported in doing what you want to do and how you want to do it.
Arms	
Function	Embracing
Left side	Resistance to embracing yourself as you are +/or attached to being a certain way +/or lack of love from your inner self.
Right side	Resistance towards a person/situation +/or attached to someone/something +/or pushing away parts of your external life/world.
Elbows	
Function	Change
Left side	Resistance to new ways of being +/or resistance to maintaining the inner status quo +/or attached to what you know.
Right side	Resistance to changing how/what you give +/or resistance to life staying the same +/or attached to your ways of doing things.

(continued)

Body parts + Causes	
Hands	
Function	Grasping
Left side	Resistance to letting go of old ways of being +/ or tendency to engage in effort to take instead of allow-in and receive.
Right side	Resistance to letting go of old ways of doing/ creating +/or holding back from giving freely +/or attached to things.
Fingers	
Function	Touch
Left side	Resistance to feeling + touching certain aspects of your inner self +/or feeling who you want to be is out of your reach +/or attached to aspects of your inner identity/sense of self.
Right side	Resistance to losing touch with what you are giving away +/or detached from what you've done/created +/or attached to parts of your life (that are being/ have been taken away).
Hips	
Function	Progress
Left side	Resistance to making progress towards new ways of being +/or attached to staying the same +/or feeling stuck within yourself +/or controlled in who you can be.
Right side	Resistance to making progress towards your goals +/or attached to getting your goals +/or feeling stuck, inactive or stagnant in what + how you are doing/creating.
Glutes	
Function	Action (or inaction)
Left side	Resistance to something that is not sitting right within you +/or attached to doing nothing +/or feeling put down +/or resistance to certain aspects of yourself that you don't want to look at sticking around.

Body parts + Causes	
Right side	Resistance to something that is not sitting right within what you are doing +/or attached to being busy +/or feeling pushed down by situation(s) +/or resistance to taking action upon certain things.
Groin	
Function	Movement
Left side	Resistance to stillness/staying where you are +/or being emotionally unmoved +/or feeling immobilized +/or lacking calm + stillness within your inner world.
Right side	Resistance to movement +/or prevented from giving fully +/or attached to moving somewhere else +/or lacking freedom in what you can do and how you can create.
Legs	
Function	Standing (or moving + kicking)
Left side	Resistance to standing up to the opinions of your inner voice +/or attached to staying where you are +/or inner self-violence.
Right side	Resistance to standing up for yourself or others +/or attached to moving somewhere +/or desire to kick out at life/world.
Thighs	
Function	Relocating
Left side	Resistance to invitations to relocate +/or attached to relocating into new ways of being.
Right side	Resistance to relocating +/or prevented from relocating +/or attached to staying where you are.
Knees	
Function	Stability (or support + protection)

(continued)

Body parts + Causes	
Knees (continued)	
Left side	Resistance to a perceived lack of inner stability +/or attached to supporting yourself +/or feeling unsafe due to perceived lack of support.
Right side	Resistance to providing stability +/or perceived loss of support +/or need to protect and brace yourself against external threat(s).
Hamstring	
Function	Extending (or stability within movement)
Left side	Resistance to perceived inner restraints +/or unstable within yourself before next step +/or contraction within your inner self.
Right side	Resistance to being stretched by what you are giving/doing +/or trying to be + do more than current ability +/or unable to extend yourself fully.
Shins	
Function	Shock absorbers
Left side	Resistance to absorbing certain shocking truth(s) about your self +/or repeated emotional shocks that have shaken your inner sense of self.
Right side	Resistance to absorbing the shock of having to give unexpectedly +/or repetitive physical shock when doing or creating in the world.
Calves	
Function	Commitment
Left side	Resistance to fully committing to who you currently are +/or inner sense of uncertainty, tentativeness + apprehension.
Right side	Resistance to committing to someone, going somewhere or do something +/or overly cautious when doing to create.

Body parts + Causes	
Ankles	
Function	Spring
Left side	Resistance to resting +/or attached to being tightly sprung to stand strong on your own +/or feeling under pressure from suppressive thoughts + feelings about who you are/should be.
Right side	Feeling strained by what you have to give +/or lacking a spring in your step in what + how you are doing/creating +/or feeling under a heavy burden from external circumstance(s).
Feet	
Function	Grounded
Left side	Lacking a solid inner foundation +/or feeling ungrounded by what you are receiving +/or saying to yourself.
Right side	Unable to remain grounded while doing + creating +/or giving more than you have to give from an unstable foundation.
Toes	
Function	Balance
Left side	Feeling unsettled by what you are giving/saying to yourself +/or lacking balance within your inner aspects of self.
Right side	Feeling unbalanced by what you are giving +/or unable to remain balanced when doing /creating what you want/need.

ORGAN DIRECTORY

This lists the common mind-based causes of conditions relating to the main organs of the body.

HOW TO USE THE ORGAN DIRECTORY

Use this directory if you have a physical condition occurring within specific organs of your body. To get the best results use the following four steps:

1. **Link the physical condition with the organ:** Scan through the list of common physical conditions to find the organ(s) that your current condition is associated with. There may be more than one, so you may need to work on more than one mind-based cause event/experience. (If your condition is not listed, then use the complete Embodying Exercise on pages 195–8)

2. **Link the organ with the mind-based cause:** Explore the mind-based causes linked with the organ(s) that your condition is associated with and find the one(s) that feel relevant to you.

3. **Find the life event/experience:** Ask yourself the recommended questions for finding the life event or experience that may be linked with the mind-based cause.

Or use the standard question: *Where in my life is this feeling or experience showing up?* If you cannot think of anything, don't overthink it. It will work as long as you experience how the mind-based cause feels.

4. **Use the Embodying Exercise (EE):** Be context aware and use steps 3 + 4 from the Embodying Exercise on page 197 to clear the conflict and embody the virtue(s) you need to bring harmony to the life event or experience that may be causing your physical condition.

TOP TIP: REST AND REVEAL

Aim to allow your mind-based cause(s) to be revealed to you by using steps 1 + 2 of the Embodying Exercise. If you have a physical condition relating to a specific organ, then use the recommended Organ Specific Calm Thoughts during your Calm Sitting with your awareness on the area of your body where your organ is located.

Organ Specific Calm Thoughts

Every organ has a recommended Calm Thought that you can use at the end of your Calm Sittings and during Calm Moments (whenever you notice that you've been thinking about the organ/condition). It is useful to have your awareness on the area of your body where the organ is located when thinking the Calm Thought. For example, if you have a heart issue, then think '*I am open, connected and in-flow with all parts of myself and life*' with your awareness on your heart area.

Organs + Mind-based causes	
Bladder	
Function	Retention
Mind-based causes	Grief, loss, fear, irritable, controlled, no control, hoarding, unwillingness to let go
Common physical conditions	Bladder infection, overactive bladder, stress urinary incontinence, urinary retention, bladder pain
Calm Thought	I am free from fear and willing to let go.
Discovery Questions	Where in my life am I experiencing grief? Who or what have I lost or am I scared of losing?
Gallbladder	
Function	Separation
Mind-based causes	Abandoned, alone, isolated, clinginess, stagnated, stuck, unable to separate good from bad
Common physical conditions	Gallbladder stones, gallbladder polyps, gallbladder cancer, severe abdominal pain, pain beneath the right shoulder blade, pain worsens after eating a meal – particularly fatty or greasy foods, pain that increases when you breathe in deeply, heartburn, indigestion, excessive gas, feeling of fullness in abdomen, shaking and chills, stools an unusual colour (lighter, clay-coloured)
Calm Thought	I am liberated by letting life's goodness in.
Discovery Questions	Where do I feel stagnated or stuck? What news can I not breakdown and make useful?
Glands	
Function	Homeostasis
Mind-based causes	Unstable, insecure, status quo challenged, unsettled, fear of the unknown, worrisome news, anxiety
Common physical conditions	Glandular fever, mumps, measles, bacterial infection, ear infection, tonsillitis, swollen glands

Organs + Mind-based causes	
Calm Thought	I am safe and feel stable as life changes.
Discovery Questions	Where in my life do I feel unstable and insecure?
	What is threatening the status quo?
Heart	
Function	Circulation
Mind-based causes	Blocked, disconnected, hurt, closed to aspects of Self, out of flow with life
Common physical conditions	Cardiovascular disease, heart attack, heart failure, blocked arteries, high or low blood pressure, angina, heart valve problem, weak heart muscles, heart infection, fast or irregular heartbeat, heart palpitations, dizziness, chest pains, shortness of breath, tiredness, swelling in legs and stomach
Calm Thought	I am open to all aspects of myself and life.
Discovery Questions	Where in my life do I feel disconnected or hurt?
	What areas of my self am I closed off to?
Large intestine	
Function	Excretion
Mind-based causes	Attachment, holding on, blocked, fear, stuck in your ways, lack mentality
Common physical conditions	Constipation, diarrhoea, intestinal gas, colon cancer, ulcerative colitis, diverticulosis
Calm Thought	I am willing to let go of what I don't need.
Discovery Questions	Who or what in my life do I feel attached to, holding on to and not willing to let go of?
	Consider people, position in workplace/society or possessions.
Liver	
Function	Purification

(continued)

Organs + Mind-based causes	
Liver (continued)	
Mind-based causes	Negativity, anger, overloaded, sluggish
Common physical conditions	Liver disease, hepatitis, cirrhosis, liver tumours, liver abscess, weight gain (liver is the main organ of fat metabolism), weakness, fatigue, weight loss, nausea, vomiting
Calm Thought	I am pure and positive about myself and life.
Discovery Questions	Where in my life do I feel overloaded with negativity? What/who do I find most irritating?
Lungs	
Function	Life force
Mind-based causes	Unsupported, scared, sadness, fear of death, restricted, suffocated
Common physical conditions	Lung cancer, asthma, chronic bronchitis and coughs, difficulty breathing, wheezing, cystic fibrosis, raspy/hoarse voice, weight loss, weakness and fatigue
Calm Thought	I am strong and supported by life.
Discovery Questions	Where in my life do I feel unsupported? What has made me feel sad or scared due to a lack of support?
Kidneys	
Function	Processing
Mind-based causes	Overthinking, fear, shock, unresolved, unsettled, unable to process events
Common physical conditions	Kidney disease, kidney failure, urinary tract infections, frequent urination, difficulty sleeping, difficulty breathing, leg cramps, vomiting, bad taste in mouth, weight loss, swelling in the legs
Calm Thought	I am able to process anything that happens.

Organs + Mind-based causes	
Discovery Questions	What unresolved thing am I overthinking about?
	What has shocked and scared me?
Pancreas	
Function	Sweetness
Mind-based causes	Numb, bored, joyless, taking on parents problems, frequently feeling let down, lacking compelling purpose
Common physical conditions	Diabetes type 1 and 2, cystic fibrosis, pancreatic cancer, pancreatitis, pancreatic pseudo cyst, enlarged pancreas, upper abdominal pain that radiates into the back, swollen or tender abdomen, nausea and vomiting, fever, increased heart rate
Calm Thought	I am grateful for and passionate about life.
Discovery Questions	When did I become numb to life?
	Where in my life am I bored or what lacks joy?
Skin	
Function	Protection
Mind-based causes	Attacked, anger, fear, separate, alone, self-critical, negativity towards self
Common physical conditions	Psoriasis, eczema, acne, skin blemishes, spots and pimples, rosacea, rashes, itching, warts, verrucas, blushing, herpes, measles, shingles, chicken pox
Calm Thought	I am secure and loveable as I am now.
Discovery Questions	Where do I feel attacked, separated or isolated?
	How am I negative towards myself?
	Consider personal appearances, abilities or lovability.
Small intestine	
Function	Absorption
Mind-based causes	Overwhelmed, unfed by life, unworthy of nourishment, rejection, resisting, unable to absorb what's happened

(continued)

Organs + Mind-based causes	
Small intestine (continued)	
Common physical conditions	Intestinal cancer, celiac disease, Crohn's disease, infection, obstructions, ulcers
Calm Thought	I am worthy of being nourished by life.
Discovery Questions	Where in my life do I feel overwhelmed?
	What am I rejecting and not absorbing?
Spleen	
Function	Protection
Mind-based causes	Powerless, defenceless, insecure, anxiety, inner conflict, defences up
Common physical conditions	Blood disorders, leukaemia, anaemia; enlarged spleen can cause hiccups or pain in the upper left quadrant of the abdomen; also compress the stomach making you feel unable to eat a full meal
Calm Thought	I am safe and secure in this loving world.
Discovery Questions	Where in my life do I feel powerless or defenceless?
	What makes me feel anxious?
	Where in my life are my defences up?
Stomach	
Function	Digestion
Mind-based causes	Incapable, fear, unable to comprehend or process, resisting indigestible event(s), anger, something eating away at you
Common physical conditions	Acid reflux, indigestion, bloating, abdominal pain, viral gastroenteritis (stomach flu), stomach ulcers, hiatal hernia, gastritis (acid imbalance), loss of appetite, nausea
Calm Thought	I am capable of comprehending calmly.
Discovery Questions	Where in my life do I feel incapable?
	What am I unable to comprehend or process?

SYSTEMS DIRECTORY

This lists the common mind-based causes of conditions relating to the 12 systems of the body.

HOW TO USE THE SYSTEMS DIRECTORY

Physical conditions occur within specific systems within the body. To use this directory, use the following four steps:

1. **Link the physical condition with the system:** Scan through the list of systems to find the one most appropriate to your current condition. There may be several systems involved so you may need to work with more than one.

2. **Link the system with the mind-based cause:** Explore the mind-based causes linked with the organ(s) that your current condition is associated with and select the ones that resonate or feel relevant.

3. **Find the life event/experience:** Ask yourself the recommended questions for finding the life event or experience that may be causing your physical conditions. If you cannot think of anything, don't overthink it. It will work as long as you experience how the mind-based cause feels.

4. **Use the Embodying Exercise to help heal:** Be context aware and use steps 3 + 4 from the Embodying Exercise on page 197 to clear the conflict and embody the virtue(s) you need to bring harmony to the life event or experience that may be causing your physical condition.

TOP TIP: REST AND REVEAL

Your mind-based causes might not seem obvious at first but try not to overthink it, just aim to allow your mind-based cause(s) to be revealed to you by using steps 1 + 2 of the Embodying Exercise or the Discovery Questions.

Systems + Mind-based causes	
Circulatory system	
Includes heart, blood vessels including arteries, veins + capillaries	
Function	Circulation + Carrying
Mind-based causes	Stuck, closed, blocked, unwilling to go with the flow, under pressure, overwhelm, hurt, lacking love, isolated, disconnected, alone, heartbreak, let down
Discovery questions	Where in my life am I experiencing a lack of flow? Where do I feel under pressure or overwhelmed? With whom do I lack connection and love? Have I had my heart broken or felt let down? Am I ignoring my body or suppressing my spiritual side?
Digestive system	
Includes mouth, oesophagus, stomach, small + large intestine, rectum, anus, liver, pancreas + gallbladder	
Function	Digestion + Nutritional absorption
Mind-based causes	Hard to stomach thoughts or events, rejection of reality, shame, distrust, unable to process or comprehend events, anger, confusion, unnourished by life, undeserving of nourishment

Systems + Mind-based causes	
Discovery questions	What have I found hard to stomach?
	What am I resisting about my current reality?
	What do I feel guilt or shame about?
	Where in my life do I feel unnourished?
	When did I decide I'm undeserving of nourishment?
	What in my life am I unable to accept, process or comprehend?

Endocrine system

Includes hypothalamus, pituitary, thyroid, pineal, parathyroid glands, thymus, adrenal glands, ovaries, testes, pancreas

Function	Regulation + Secretion
Mind-based causes	Unable to manage life, un-giving, status quo challenged, controlled, out of control, unbalanced, confused, irritated, exhausted by never-ending effort, pressure to perform, sexual confusion, conflicted messages
Discovery questions	What in my life am I unable to manage?
	Where in my life do I feel controlled and I'm not able to control myself? What am I confused about?
	What is requiring a never-ending effort?
	Do I have any sexual confusion?
	What am I conflicted about?

Immune system

Includes lymph nodes, lymphocytes, organs that produce cells + blood vessels

Function	Protection + Elimination
Mind-based causes	Attacked, vulnerable, unable to fight, unprotected, exposed, threatened, controlled, inner conflict, harshness towards self
Discovery questions	What do I feel unable to fight?
	What is making me feel vulnerable or exposed?
	Where in my life do I feel threatened or under attack?
	In what ways am I being way too hard on myself?

(continued)

Systems + Mind-based causes	
Integumentary system	
Includes nails, hair, skin, some exocrine glands	
Function	Environmental protection
Mind-based causes	Need to defend, closed off, alone, rejection of environment, anger, separation, external threats, bullied, invaded, violated
Discovery questions	What do I feel I need to defend against? Who in my life have I felt bullied by? Where in my life am I experiencing separation? What have I been rejecting or am I closed off to? Where in my life do I feel judged from external sources?
Lymphatic system	
Includes spleen, appendix, tonsils, thymus gland, lymph nodes, ducts + vessels	
Function	Collection + Transportation
Mind-based causes	Trapped, stuck, alone, stagnant, blocked, negativity, unmoved, inactivity, fear, hiding, excluded, external threats, lacking flow + movement in life
Discovery questions	Where do I feel stuck in my life? Where in my life is there a build up of negativity? What's stagnant? Where am I resisting moving forward? What am I hiding from?
Muscular system	
Includes 700 named muscles that consist of skeletal tissue, blood vessels, tendons + nerves	
Function	Strength + Movement
Mind-based causes	Weak, vulnerable, unable to cope, scared of own power, worry, tense, overthinking, unsupported, heavy responsibility, fear, trapped, stuck, unable to move

Systems + Mind-based causes	
Discovery questions	Where in my life am I suppressing my power? Where do I feel unable to cope? What is making me feel weak/powerless? What is making me feel trapped or unable to move freely?

Nervous system

Includes brain, spinal cord and nerves that branch off from spinal cord + send messages to the entire body

Function	Interpretation + Communication
Mind-based causes	Unable to comprehend, unable to respond, overwhelmed by the sensory experience, conflict, confusion, tension, blame, on-going stressful situation, negative internal dialogue, moaning, complaining + being pessimistic
Discovery questions	What am I finding it hard to respond to? What is making me feel overwhelmed? What am I unable to process or understand? Who am I blaming? What on-going stressful situation am I resisting? What do I often moan, complain and think negatively about?

Reproductive system

Includes testes, prostate gland + penis (males), ovaries, uterus, breasts + vagina (females)

Function	Reproduction + Cycle of life
Mind-based causes	Resistance to create, low confidence, guilt, shame, invaded, unsafe, embarrassed, sexual confusion, dislike, critical, resistance to being like parents or experiencing what parents did, fear of parenthood, holding back from giving, nothing left to give resistance to receive, concern for child

(continued)

Systems + Mind-based causes	
Reproductive system (continued)	
Discovery questions	Where in my life are there relationship hurts?
	Where in my life am I playing the victim?
	What do I feel unable to create?
	What has made me feel invaded, dirty or wrong?
	What's made me feel really embarrassed?
	Where in my life do I feel repulsed?
	Where in my life do I feel criticized or am I being overly critical?
	What fears do I have surrounding being a parent?
	Am I resistant to being like a parent or experiencing what they did?
	Am I concerned over a child's safety?
Respiratory system	
Includes throat, trachea (windpipe), sinuses, nasal cavity, lungs	
Function	Supplying + Sustaining life
Mind-based causes	Resisting life, lack of passion +/or purpose, depression, lack of compelling future, having to be own life support, alone, undeserving, not giving yourself what you need, feeling suffocated, isolation, guilt, grief, fear of death, shock
Discovery questions	What am I resisting in my life?
	Where in my life do I feel suffocated?
	When did I decide I couldn't/shouldn't support myself?
	What do I need but am not giving to myself?
	Where in my life do I feel wronged?
	When did I decide that I'm undeserving?
	What do I feel is irreversibly wrong with me?
	What has caused me to fear for my survival?

Systems + Mind-based causes	
Skeletal system	
Includes bones, cartilage, tendons ligaments, teeth	
Function	Structure + Support
Mind-based causes	Inflexibility, closed-mindedness, refusal to stand up for yourself, unable to support self, unforgiveness, hate, bitterness, judgemental
Discovery questions	Where am I being inflexible? In what way(s) am I being closed-minded? Where in my life am I not standing up for myself? Where do I feel unable to support myself? What do I feel bitterness about or am I being overly judgemental?
Urinary system	
Includes bladder, kidneys, ureters, urethra	
Function	Cleansing + Controlling
Mind-based causes	Negativity, holding on, holding back, angry, bitter, blocked, unbalanced, impure, unclean, out of control, controlling, marking territory, invasion of your space
Discovery questions	Where in my life am I holding onto negativity? What in my life is out of balance? What am I feeling upset about? Where am I unable to separate the good from the bad? Where do I feel my personal space is being invaded?

SENSES DIRECTORY

This offers guidance on the common mind-based causes of issues relating to your five senses.

HOW TO USE THE SENSES DIRECTORY

The Senses Directory includes the following:

- Ears – hearing/auditory

- Eyes – sight/visual

- Nose – smell/olfactory

- Receptors – touch/somatic

- Tongue – taste/gustatory

Within the context of your body adapting to keep you safe, survive and highlight aspects of your life that are in disharmony, the senses are highly symbolic. For each of the senses, if they have changed at a certain time in your life, then consider the descriptions provided in the directory and answer the corresponding questions in relation to what's been going on in your life using the following three steps.

1. **Read the common reasons:** Scan through list of senses to find the one most appropriate to your current condition. Read the common reasons for issues relating to the sense

2. **Ask the Discovery Questions:** Answer the questions to find your mind–body cause. Remember; don't worry if you cannot think of any specific event. It will work as long as you experience how the mind-based cause feels.

3. **Use Embodying Exercise:** Be context aware and use steps 3 + 4 from the Embodying Exercise on page 197 to clear the conflict and embody the virtue(s) you need to bring harmony to that may be causing your physical condition.

Senses + Mind-based causes	
Ears	
Sense	Hearing
Function	Receiving
Mind-based causes	Hearing can link with your willingness to hear certain things and receive certain information from other people or during life events/experiences.
	Hearing tends to be reduced when you are resisting or rejecting what you have heard or are currently hearing. This can include not wanting to listen to your own inner voice. Hearing problems can also stem from being attached to hearing certain people or things, for example, the loss of a loved one and therefore no longer being able to hear their voice.
Discovery Questions	Who or what do I not want to listen to?
	This may be a family member or partner. It may also relate to news you received that you rejected and did not want to hear.
	Where in my life am I not listening to my inner voice?

(continued)

Senses + Mind-based causes	
Eyes	
Sense	Sight
Function	Perceiving
Mind-based causes	Capacity to see the past, present and future clearly. If there are certain things you don't want to look at or cannot see/imagine, then your eyes can adapt. Vision tends to become short-sighted when you cannot or do not want to see far into your future i.e. you do not have a compelling future or are resisting what might happen. Vision tends to become long-sighted when there are things in your close proximity that you don't want to see, look at or imagine. There's a tendency in longsighted people to want to ignore the past or present and focus more on the future.
Discovery Questions	What in my life don't I want to look at? What am I imagining about my possible future that I don't like to visualize? What has happened to make me want to ignore the past or focus on the future more?
Nose	
Sense	Smell
Function	Selectivity
Mind-based causes	Smell is links with selectivity. If you are not being selective in certain areas of your life then your sense of smell can be impacted. Your body is reflecting your compromised selectivity by lowering the sense of smell. Or if you are finding it hard to decide between different options then your smell can become over-sensitive. Your body is trying to help you to be better able to select between options.

Senses + Mind-based causes	
Discovery Questions	Where in my life do I need to be more selective?
	Where in my life am I finding it hard to choose between different options?
Receptors	
Sense	Touch
Function	Connection
Mind-based causes	Touch is about your connection with your self, others and life. If you are resisting anything you are currently connected to or attached to staying connected, your sense of touch can be impacted. If you are resisting, touch can be reduced and if you are overly attached you can become hypersensitive.
	Touch can also be impacted if there is something in your life that you are finding hard to grasp. You may also experience an inability to physically feel if you are unwilling to feel certain emotions. When this happens your body is mirroring your mind's unwillingness to feel by reducing its sense of touch.
Discovery Questions	Who or what in my life do I feel disconnected from?
	Who or what in my life do I have a resistance to being touched by and/or touching?
	What in my life am I finding hard to grasp and/or feel I've lost a grasp of?
	What emotions am I suppressing?
Tongue	
Sense	Taste
Function	Discriminating

(continued)

Senses + Mind-based causes	
Tongue (continued)	
Mind-based causes	Your taste helps you to discriminate between good and bad, sweet and sour and, in turn, conclude whether or not you want to swallow something. Hard-to-swallow events can impact your taste, your ability to create saliva and your ability to physically swallow, so the throat can also be linked with taste conflicts. Taste can also become compromised if there are distasteful things in your past or present. These events or experiences may have left a bad taste in your mouth.
Discovery Questions	Where in my life am I finding it hard to differentiate between good/bad, right/wrong? What in my life have I found distasteful? What areas of my life have turned sour? What have I found hard to swallow?

CONDITIONS DIRECTORY

This lists the common mind-based causes of 101 physical conditions.

HOW TO USE THE CONDITIONS DIRECTORY

This directory shares the mind-based causes for 101 physical conditions. To use it, engage GAAWO and read the common causes by feeling them from awareness. This will enable you to recognize the mind-based causes that resonate with you the most. Then ask: *Where has this feeling of experience shown up in my life?* before using steps 3 + 4 of the Embodying Exercise on page 197.

You may notice that there are multiple emotional causes for each condition. Everyone is unique so conditions can have a range of possible mind–body connection causes. You want to only focus on the reasons that resonate with you.

Condition Specific Calm Thoughts

Every condition has a recommended Condition-Specific Calm Thought that you can use during your Calm Sittings (before ending with I AM HEALED) and Calm Moments (whenever you notice you've been thinking about your condition or throughout your day whenever you remember to do it). If your condition relates to a specific area of your body then feel free to put your awareness on that area as you think the Calm Thought. For example, if you have acid reflux and you feel discomfort in your throat, you want to think '*I am accepting of myself and life*' with your awareness on your throat area.

Based upon this Conditions Directory, I've recorded a series of guided meditations that can give you extra support to help heal the mind-based causes of specific conditions. Please visit www.sandynewbigging.com for track listings and to download them.

Conditions + Mind-based causes	
Acne	Negativity towards self, comparison, feeling less than, lacking self-love, unaccepted, nervousness, unworthiness, unresolved pubescent event(s), perfectionistic, controlling, anger, 'There's something wrong with me'
Calm Thought	I am lovingly gentle towards myself.
Acid reflux	Certain thing(s) hard to digest in relation to what you've witnessed and/or experienced, rejecting news, fear, anxiety, communication difficulties, anger about injustice, guilt and shame surrounding past action(s), self-doubt, acidic thinking
Calm Thought	I am accepting of myself and life.
Allergies	Anger, unfriendly environment, unprotected, powerless, scared about getting in trouble, difficulty relaxing, unresolved hurt, blame/victim mentality, feeling controlled, unclear boundaries
Calm Thought	I am friendly with the unfamiliar and responsible for how I respond to life.

Conditions + Mind-based causes	
Anaemia	Scared of what life might bring, expectation of difficulties arising, uneasy, worrisome thinking, unable to cope, questioning of abilities, feeling someone/something has 'drained the life' out of you, giving out without allowing yourself to receive back
Calm Thought	I am joyfully facing life and assuming the best.
Appendicitis	Lacking inspiration in life, helpless, scared of what might happen, stuck unable to get away from toxic situation, angry, disappointed, loyalty conflict, let down by life, too hard on yourself
Calm Thought	I am grateful for what I have and empowered to bring in even better.
Arthritis	Holding on, fixed ideas, identity attachment, anger, grief, resentment, giving out without getting back what you need, 'other people's goals more important than mine', unforgiveness, unresolved childhood rejections, unhappy with life but not doing anything about improving things
Calm Thought	I am able to let go, let in the new and take action to be happy.
Asthma	Fear of death, unsupported in life, unable to cope, suppression of self, picking up on the stress and tension of parent or person close to you, undeserving of good things, need to prove worth, people pleasing to get love
Calm Thought	I am supported, deserving of the good and willing to say no when required.

(continued)

237

Conditions + Mind-based causes	
Atherosclerosis	Feeling blocked, hard relationships, narrow-minded (but wouldn't want to admit it), limited range of feeling, disconnected from multifaceted self (for example, too physical not enough spiritual), not going with the flow, separate, isolation
Calm Thought	I am open-minded and -hearted and connected to my entire self.
Athlete's foot	Taking on-board someone else's stale thinking/ways, anger at a perceived lack of love, feeling restricted and prevented from freely moving forward, looking outside for permission to act
Calm Thought	I am accepted for who I am and free to move forward with fresh ideas.
Auto-immune	Vulnerable, feeling attacked and/or under-threat, inner conflict, unable to fight or run from external problem/threat, unsure who/what to trust, shutting down to protect, 'world is a dangerous place' mentality, overprotective, being hard on yourself
Calm Thought	I am safe and protected within myself and the world.
Back pain (lower)	Unsupported, unable to support self, resistance +/or attachment to support others, unsafe, weak, vulnerable, incapable
Calm Thought	I am supported and willing and able to support myself and others.
Back pain (middle)	Disconnected from self, others +/or life force, threat from unseen source, hurt
Calm Thought	I am connected to all aspects of myself.

Conditions + Mind-based causes	
Back pain (upper)	World on your shoulders, people pleasing, carrying expectations, taking on other people's issues, unresolved pressing problem, suppressed, resistance to carry heavy problems/emotionally heavy people, attached to being carried
Calm Thought	I am blessed by being able to carry myself and other people lightly.
Bacterial infection	Tired, fragile, vulnerable to being negatively impacted by other people and external events, feeling unloved/unsupported, stuck in a situation, angry at unfair treatment
Calm Thought	I am strong and inwardly reliant and able to move into a happier space.
Bad breath	Personal space being invaded, desire to create separation, loner, past hurts leading to self-isolating tendencies, disgust towards inner voice
Calm Thought	I am open to being close and to feeling connected to myself and others.
Bleeding gums	Unspoken insecurities, unnourished by others and life, angry and alone with a lack of support
Calm Thought	I am secure and supported by life.
Burping (and also sneezing)	Unspoken thoughts about things you dislike, rejection of ideas, unresolved conflict(s) in relation to what you have recently consumed
Calm Thought	I am free to speak my mind.
Cancer	Resistance to life, hurt, bitterness, anger, victim mentality, unforgiveness, guilt, grief, regret, perceived lack of love, out of control, unresolved past hurts, invaded, hiding and resistance to true feelings, attached to a different life

(continued)

Conditions + Mind-based causes	
Cancer (continued)	
Calm Thought	I am free to forgive and I love life in a loving and compassionate world.
Candida	Vulnerable, invaded, untrusting, imbalance between taking and giving, feeding off others, doubt, anger towards an irritating person/situation
Calm Thought	I am able to forgive and feed my own needs.
Celiac disease	Judgemental, good vs. bad thinking, attached to good, resisting bad, sensitive to external influences, unable to cope with criticism, self-dislike, unable to digest being unheard/uncared about, hiding true thoughts/feelings, unseen
Calm Thought	I am accepting and allowing, and release the need for others to nourish me.
Chronic pain	Anger, resentment, resisting emotions, not being honest or feeling true feelings, things left unsaid +/or unfelt, unforgivingness
Calm Thought	I am free to feel and speak my feelings.
Colds	Overwhelmed, overworking, fast-paced non-stop living, uncertainty, confusion, escaping environmental negativity
Calm Thought	I am safe when I slow down and rest.
Cold sores	Feeling run-down, uncommunicative, concerns around being accepted, awkwardness, feeling controlled by others and let down by life
Calm Thought	I am accepted for who I am and able to feel comfortable when showing myself.
Colitis	Hurt, helpless, sad, confused, 'what's the point?' mentality, want external help instead of helping yourself, unable to process or comprehend what's happened, holding onto to painful past

Conditions + Mind-based causes	
Calm Thought	I am free from past hurts and able to help myself heal and be happy.
Conjunctivitis	Fear of what might happen, worry, resisting the possibility others see you in a negative light
Calm Thought	I am loved always, with love being the unseen connector within all of life.
Constipation	Undecided, holding on, fear of not having enough, ungratefulness, loss, resisting change, hoarding, giving what you need, uncomfortable to receive, stuck in worrisome thinking pattern, scared about what might happen
Calm Thought	I am grateful for having enough and make courageous decisions.
Cough	Feeling unseen +/or unheard, barking at life, feeling left out, unable to ask for what you want or need, ignoring issues, irritation at self and others, inaction
Calm Thought	I am included, important and able to make positive changes.
Dandruff	Feeling sucked dry by pressures, people +/or responsibilities, too many things to do, overworking, people pleasing, hiding true feelings relating to how stressed you feel, suffering in silence
Calm Thought	I am capable of meeting the demands of my day and do what's comfortable.
Deafness	Resistance +/or rejection to what you are hearing/have heard, more interested in your inner world than external world, overloaded by negativity, unresolved past events where you've heard upsetting things, feeling unheard and/or controlled by others, unwilling to receive guidance

(continued)

Conditions + Mind-based causes	
Deafness (continued)	
Calm Thought	I am receiving my inner and outer world loud and clear.
Dermatitis	Highly critical towards self and others, anger, feeling concerned and stressed about external life and circumstances, rejection of environment, feeling used +/or violated
Calm Thought	I am accepting of my world and calm with circumstances.
Depression	Thinking about life instead of living, lack of compelling purpose, pointlessness, resistance to feeling fully to the point of numbness, unseen, overthinking, 'surviving life is difficult' thoughts
Calm Thought	I deserve the good in life and let 'what is' be good enough.
Diabetes	Lacking sweetness, numb, bored, taking on parents problems, frequently feeling left down, self-suppression, wanting more from life but unsure how to get it, fear, lacking compelling purpose, judgement instead of joy, effort to exist
Calm Thought	I am the sweetness I want and worthy of being myself fully.
Diarrhoea	Emotional upset, strategy for getting away/avoiding, angry at being told what to do, perceived lack of choice, escaping, uncertainly surrounding choices, fear, rejecting before you are rejected
Calm Thought	I am free to choose what feels safe and do what I want.
Diverticulitis	Unexpressed non-acceptance, anger and agitation about what life has given you, resistance to 'what is' and attachment to something else happening, controlling, 'My way or no way'

Conditions + Mind-based causes	
Calm Thought	I am accepting of what is and open to new ways of being and doing.
Dizziness	Imbalanced, ungrounded, loss of stability, don't know where you stand, too in your head, disconnected from body, resistance to uncertainty
Calm Thought	I am grounded within my still stable Self.
Dystonia	Constricting inner power, scared of own strength, shame about things you shouldn't have done, scared of hurting others, conflict towards completion, 'I can't do it' attitude
Calm Thought	I am free to use my strength and commit to completing.
Earache	Not listening to inner voice, rejection to what you are hearing from external sources, protecting yourself by trying to ignore what you are hearing, closed to other opinions and ideas, annoyance
Calm Thought	I am open to hearing opinions knowing I am a good person.
Eczema	Sadness-based anger, alone in the world, skin trying to find lost connection, isolated, irritated, emotionally sensitive, unstable without physical contact, separation anxiety
Calm Thought	I am calm and connected.
Endometriosis	Closed off to love, need for pity, sexual shame, intimacy vulnerability, anger, feeling misunderstood or undervalued, attachment or resistance to past sexual partner(s), resistance to rejection
Calm Thought	I am open to connecting deeply.

(continued)

Conditions + Mind-based causes	
Fatigue	Unable to fight or get away from something stressful/scary +/or negative, feeling suppressed, overwhelmed, chronic resistance, rejecting life before it rejects you again
Calm Thought	I am accepting of my inner power.
Flatulence	Difficulty digesting inner thoughts or external events, inner concern, keeping things to yourself, feeling undecided
Calm Thought	I am able to make decisions and digest what's happened and happening.
Fungal infections	Stale thinking, acting against your inner knowing/heart, relationship secrets that make you feel unclean, holding onto a past that no longer serves you today
Calm Thought	I am fresh in my thinking and free of the past.
Gallstones	Unresolved hurt(s), loss, feeling like you should have done more with your life, anger towards self, unforgiveness
Calm Thought	I am at peace with what's happened and capable of creating.
Glandular fever	Feeling unwanted, anger and hurt towards a perceived lack of love, 'If nobody else cares why should I?' mentality, tired of trying to prove lovability, dejected, unable to express, resistance to feeling inner emotions fully
Calm Thought	I am loved and wanted and am willing to feel and be me.
Haemorrhoids	Holding on, emotionally uncomfortable with choices you've made, unsure what to do next, feeling under pressure, unforgiving towards self and others
Calm Thought	I am at peace with past choices and open to knowing and doing what's best.

Conditions + Mind-based causes	
Hair loss	Feeling vulnerable, unprotected, fear of the unknown, prolonged stress, underlying frustrations, resistance to feminine aspects of self
Calm Thought	I am safe and calmly face anything that comes my way.
Hay fever	Environmental threats, rejecting or questioning your place on Earth, guilt, resistance to receive, resisting location, lacking space, fighting feelings
Calm Thought	I am happy where I am with space to think, feel and be still.
Headaches	Something on your mind, overthinking, denial, guilt, shame, regret, self-suppression, deserving of punishment, invasion of space, angry thoughts
Calm Thought	I am accepting of myself and life.
Heart disease	Hurt, closed-off, sadness, ignoring the needs of the physical, emotional +/or spiritual aspects of your self, divided, disconnected, hard relationships
Calm Thought	I am open to all aspects of myself.
Herpes	Belief of being 'bad', sexual shame, deserving of punishment, needing excuse to avoid intimacy, feeling used, violated or unclean
Calm Thought	I am a good person with pure intentions.
Hives	Angry and irritated with self, others +/or life, overwhelmed by feelings +/or circumstances, fear, helplessness
Calm Thought	I am calm and at peace with myself, others and my environment.

(continued)

Conditions + Mind-based causes	
Hyperhidrosis	Anger, irritated, unfairness, resistance to being in the hot seat and the centre of attention, need to mentally and emotionally cool down, unresolved shock, scared of own strength
Calm Thought	I am cool with being the centre of attention and calm about the past.
Hypertension	Resistance, worry, anxiety, belief the world is a dangerous place, controlling, not safe to relax, unwilling to let go, attached to things happening 'my way'
Calm Thought	I am at peace with how the world is
Hyperthyroidism	Resistance to maintaining status quo, need to get going, nervous tension, anxious, irritability, feeling held back +/or being/doing what you need to do, desire to move forward but feeling blocked, pressure from responsibilities, questioning readiness to support self, felt forced to grow up to quickly.
Calm Thought	I am free to make progress towards my purpose at a peaceful pace.
Hypotension	Drained by attachments, not getting what you want, tired of trying, negativity around own abilities and purpose, belief that nobody is there for me, what's the point if nobody cares?
Calm Thought	I am passionate about going for my purpose without needing it.
Hypothyroidism	Unsafe, unable to cope, weak, vulnerable, too much to deal with, resisting a perceived lack of support in past or present, resistance to responsibilities, need to retreat to protect and feel safe, 'Life is hard', 'I can't do this' +/or 'What's the point?'

Conditions + Mind-based causes	
Calm Thought	I am capable of coping with life and more supported than I may think.
Infections	Feeling vulnerable to external attack, overpowered by external influences, low defences, unable to cope, anger towards nobody noticing your difficulties, prolonged pressure to perform, tired of trying so hard
Calm Thought	I am able to cope and give myself permission to be at ease and enjoy life.
Infertility	Imbalance between masculine and feminine energies, resistance to receiving +/or creating, feeling inadequate, unresolved past fears around falling pregnant, unresolved issues with parent(s), avoidance of and fears around making the same mistakes your parents did or having similar experiences
Calm Thought	I am balanced in my ability to give and receive and thankful for what my parents have taught me.
Influenza	Too much external negativity, weak and vulnerable, running on empty, finding it hard to carry responsibilities, wanting to get away from it all, needing to justify taking time off/get away
Calm Thought	I am free to take time for myself to rest and let go of extra responsibilities.
Insomnia	Not safe to switch off, need to stay alert, ignoring unresolved events, undeserving of the reward of rest, over-compromising, unheard heart
Calm Thought	I am at peace with being peaceful.

(continued)

Conditions + Mind-based causes	
Irritable bowel syndrome (IBS)	Irritated, unable to process, comprehend or understand, fear, emotional upset, untrusting, holding onto out-of-date thinking, uncertainty conflict between needing to let go/get away and holding on to what no longer serves, attached
Calm Thought	I am clear-minded, light-hearted and pursue my purpose with positivity.
Itching	Anger, irritation, hot-headedness, self-punishment, shame, hiding secrets that sit below the surface, worry, angst
Calm Thought	I am secure within the skin I'm in.
Kidney infection	Feeling upset, bitter, impure, holding onto negativity, fear, unsafe, perceived threats to your boundaries, low confidence, powerless due to exhaustion, tired of trying
Calm Thought	I am confident and able to maintain healthy boundaries.
Kidney stone	Fear-based anger, lacking trust, need to be hard to protect and feel safe, set in your ways, focused on the past to the detriment of the present and the future, feeling 'less than', pressure to perform
Calm Thought	I am trusting that I am safe and take positive action into new territory.
Lips (dry/cracked)	Unconfident, scared to look stupid, be rejected and make a fool of yourself, nervousness, questioning abilities to deliver, uncertainty around what you are saying
Calm Thought	I am carefree around what people think and believe in my abilities to deliver.

Conditions + Mind-based causes	
Menopausal symptoms	Buying into cultural beliefs around aging, suppressed anger and frustration, resisting loss of youthfulness +/or desirability
Calm Thought	I am loving life as an ageless goddess.
Migraines	Resistance to unfair events, guilt, regret, shame, self-punishment, invasion of space, shutting the world out, unable to ask for what you need, safer to be sick than face the world, unable to cope, denial, grief
Calm Thought	I am capable with a good heart.
Mouth ulcer	Anger eating away at you, not expressing personal opinions, resistance to what you are thinking or saying, holding in frustration, attached to old thinking habits that promote problems rather than peace
Calm Thought	I am open to new perspectives that allow me to be at peace.
Mumps	Overthinking, ignoring/going against inner knowing, unable to say what you think, instability, status quo challenged, uncertain, fear of the unknown
Calm Thought	I am comfortable with uncertainly and can rely on my inner knowing.
Myalgic encephalopathy (ME)	Resistance towards and fighting life, viewing life as a struggle, anger due to feelings of unfairness, unexpressed thoughts/feelings, retreating from responsibilities, under pressure to fulfil commitments, unable to fight or get aware from stressful person/situation
Calm Thought	I am free to be and do what I want and at peace with what life brings.

(continued)

Conditions + Mind-based causes	
Nausea	Confusion, constant questioning, feeling out of control, unable to receive what you want/need, rejection of information +/or an unwanted experience, holding a poisonous perspective, sick to the stomach by something or someone, ungrounded
Calm Thought	I am stable in what I know is right.
Numbness	Unwilling to feel feelings fully, untrusting of instincts and intuition, unresolved emotions from the past, detached from aspects of yourself
Calm Thought	I am willing to feel fully and trust my instincts and intuitions.
Osteoporosis	Inflexibility, rigid thinking, fixed ideas, unwilling to change, lack of structure, unable to support self, weak from supporting others, feeling inferior, bitterness, hate, resistance to standing up for yourself +/or attachment to external source of structure/support
Calm Thought	I am flexible and stand strongly in love.
Parasites	Negativity, powerless, feeling people/events are feeding off your energy, invaded, unclear boundaries, imbalance between giving and receiving (less gained than given), imbalance
Calm Thought	I am empowered by having balance between giving and receiving.
Parkinson's disease	Moving fearfully through life, unresolved past events that caused panic, stuck energy, feeling stuck in situations, conflicted between what's right for you and what's best for others, hiding and suppressing your true feelings
Calm Thought	I am free and express my true feelings.

Conditions + Mind-based causes	
Period pains	Resistance to not being pregnant, grief, anger, unresolved emotions relating to around the time in life when periods first started, resistance to female roles and responsibilities, 'not fair' mentality
Calm Thought	I am at peace with letting go.
Pneumonia	Unsupported by life, looking outside for sustenance, alone, isolated, drained by daily duties, unwilling or unable to face life challenges, feeling restricted, closed
Calm Thought	I am supported by life and able to stand strongly when faced with challenges.
Polymyalgia rheumatica	Rigid thinking, unwilling to accept other viewpoints, frustrated that your viewpoints are unheard, not listening to or acting upon inner voice, carrying heavy responsibilities, 'what's the point' mentality, feeling controlled, unable to make progress towards what you want
Calm Thought	I am open-minded, share my opinions without attachment and am able to make progress.
Prostate	Feeling taken over or controlled, conflicts around getting older, intrusion of work or personal space, status quo challenged
Calm Thought	I am secure with my space in the world.
Psoriasis	Feeling bullied, unprotected, vulnerable, fear, need extra thick line of defence, unresolved near-death experience, hurt
Calm Thought	I am protected and powerful.
Raynaud's disease	Ignoring/closed off to aspects of yourself and life, not going with the flow, isolated, disconnected, alone
Calm Thought	I am going with the flow and open to all aspects of myself and life.

(continued)

Conditions + Mind-based causes	
Shingles	Highly sensitive, unable to cope and/or keep up with demands, concerns relating to circumstances, environmental fears, masculine/feminine imbalance (depending on side of body the symptoms are showing – see Body Part Directory, pages 209–15)
Calm Thought	I am at peace within myself and comfortable with circumstances.
Sinusitis	Frustration towards self, others +/or environmental concerns, feeling blocked with a desire to run away, facing life with a lack of tenderness, unable to select/choose between multiple options, indecision, fear of getting it wrong due to unresolved emotions relating to perceive past mistakes
Calm Thought	I am at peace with the world, trusting of my instincts and choose what's right.
Snoring	Not feeling heard, things on your mind that remain unsaid, holding back from taking the action you know you need to take, fear of the new, stuck in ways
Calm Thought	I am free to be and do what I want.
Sore throat	Not speaking truth, holding thoughts and feelings in, 'What I have to say doesn't matter or make a difference'
Calm Thought	I am free to speak my mind.
Stomach pain + bloating	Indigestible news, unable to process or understand, things unsaid/unfelt, suppression of true thoughts/feelings
Calm Thought	I am welcoming of unexpected news and I am honest with myself and others.

Conditions + Mind-based causes	
Stye (eye)	Losing sight of someone or something you love dearly, feeling separated, loss of love, confusion, scared, disorientated, unresolved anger and disappointment
Calm Thought	I am open to love from new sources.
Teeth grinding	Responsibilities playing on your mind, bitten off more than you can chew, worry, anger, hidden desire to bite out, indecision, processing something
Calm Thought	I am clear on what to do and will do it with calmness and confidence.
Thrush	Angry and irritated towards self about past decisions and actions, upset with partner, self-judgemental, self-critical, feeling invaded by other people's ideas, opinions or needs, ignoring own needs
Calm Thought	I am at peace with my past decisions.
Tinnitus	Rejection of what you are saying to yourself or what you have heard, isolation, lost in your own world, resistance to silence or sound
Calm Thought	I am engaged with life and eager to hear.
Tonsillitis	Not speaking truth, protecting secrets, guilt, fear of being found out, need to put defences up, suppressing self, feeling frustrated +/or stifled
Calm Thought	I am imperfectly perfect like everyone else.

(continued)

Conditions + Mind-based causes	
Tumours	Hurts, emotional wounds, unresolved trauma +/or shock, inner conflict caused by jealousy towards others and not believing it's possible for you +/or not feeling deserving/worthy *Also explore the other directories regarding the body area, organ +/or system in which the tumour(s) are located for possible mind-based causes.*
Calm Thought	I am worthy of calm and completeness.
Ulcers	Something eating away at you, bitter, acidic thinking/feeling, pushing down, resentment in your responsibilities
Calm Thought	I am allowing of life.
Warts	Anger due to an event that made you feel scared, extra thick defence against singular event, feeling incapable, ugly
Calm Thought	I am at peace with no need to protect.
Water retention	Relationship problems, sadness, overflowing with emotions, feeling stagnant, need for the new, not making the changes you know you need to make, holding back from being happy
Calm Thought	I am in flow with my feelings and open to knowing how to be happy.
Weight gain	Unprotected, unsafe, unfamiliar +/or unfriendly environment(s), no control, hiding, withholding true feelings, unable to cope, loss of comfort, harsh self-speak that body needs to protect itself from, lack of self-love/acceptance
Calm Thought	I am surrendering to how my delicious destiny is being revealed to me.

Conditions + Mind-based causes	
Weight loss	Dissatisfaction, unfed by life, undeserving of nourishment, cry for help, controlling, vulnerable, unresolved resistance to lack of support, unable to take what you need, unworthy of the good, shame, 'It's my fault' mentality.
Calm Thought	I am nourished and deserving of the good in life.
Verrucas	Angry at self, guilt, something eating away at you, secret(s), needing to take action steps but letting fear stop you, feeling ungrounded due to the confusion arising from the multiple options available
Calm Thought	I am at peace with myself and am willing to do what I know I need to do.
Viruses	External environmental issues (making you feel vulnerable, invaded, attacked, unfairly 'got at'), under pressure, scared and/or stuck, feeling unable to fight, unprotected, living in a state of high alert, inability to relax, inner unease
Calm Thought	I am safe and protected and can keep calm amid challenging circumstances.
Voice loss	Unheard, what you say doesn't matter, powerless to make a positive difference, ignoring your inner voice, feeling unable to fully express your feelings
Calm Thought	I am heard and know what I feel is important even if others don't appear to listen.
Yeast infections	Feeling invaded by other people's ideas, opinions or needs, ignoring own needs, lack of self-love and respect
Calm Thought	I am able to think whatever I want.

TOP TIP: NEED MORE HELP?

If your condition is not listed, then explore the Body Parts, Organ, Systems and Senses Directories for potential causes. If you are unsure or feel uncomfortable working on what you find on your own, then please contact a Body Calm Coach (see Next Steps on pages 263–4 for details).

HOME TO THE HEART

I began this book by sharing the Body Calm philosophy, which is based upon the simple yet powerful premise that the purpose of life is to live fully and completely. I went on to suggest that health becomes compromised when there is conflict within ourselves and towards life, due to the chronic stress caused by the constant push-pull dynamic of resistance and attachment.

To end the book I want to clarify what it means to live 'fully and completely' – so that you avoid any confusion or unnecessary self-imposed stress. When you first explore this philosophy, it can appear that you have to engage in lots of effort to create more and achieve more so that you may eventually live fully and completely. However, this is not what I'm suggesting.

Life is already full.

Life lacks nothing. The here and now, when engaged with fully and completely, is already rich and continuously giving you all that you need to fulfil your purpose. So please do not feel under any pressure to perform. You do not need to engage in doing extra to get more. Instead, you just need to be consciously aware enough to experience 'what is' and remove any mind-based barriers that stand in the way of you experiencing your Self and life fully and completely.

Have you found that you've been fighting your feelings or resisting certain life events or experiences? Have you seen areas of your life in which you've not been listening to your heart or been lacking an awareness of the calm context of life? To return to radiant health and real happiness, Body Calm aims to move you towards a state of liberated living in which you are free to feel and experience all aspects of human life.

With conscious awareness, anything can be experienced in its entirety, without fear, stress or suffering, whether you are washing the dishes, taking a walk or talking to a friend and irrespective of whether you are facing an operation, have got lots on at work or are dealing with debt. The content of what's happening need not be detrimental to your health and happiness, as long as you are Self-aware and embody virtues anytime you notice yourself stressing. Remember, it is resistance to feeling and experiencing fully and attachment that causes conflict. With the right attitude and awareness, mundane tasks become magical and challenging physical conditions and circumstances can be invitations to wake up and live more fully. By relating to life in this way, you enjoy greater harmony, and health and lots of happiness, too.

A COMPREHENSIVE HEALTH AND HEALING STRATEGY

Adopting a self-healing strategy that combines both conventional and alternative methods makes good sense. I have huge respect for doctors and often find myself in awe of the many marvels of modern medicine. There is also ever-increasing evidence proving the common-sense benefits of quality nutrition, staying hydrated and keeping fit with regular exercise. So I'm not suggesting that you should *only* meditate. Rather, I urge you to use meditation and embodying as aids to healing and life-long wellness – and as part of an overall healthier lifestyle that can make you more fulfilled, too.

Having gained an appreciation of the oneness within your mind, body, soul and life, if you happen to have a physical condition, use Body Calm to harness the power of the mind–body connection to help healing. Let your body be a trusted friend and one of your most important teachers – especially now you know how to interpret its many meaningful messages.

With the right mind-set, you can use ill health to highlight any areas in your inner and outer life where you need to clear conflict and restore harmony.

By using the Body Calm meditation technique daily to rest, aid recovery and deepen your relationship with the inner presence of calm consciousness, and also, by using the Embodying Exercise and Body Calm Directories anytime you notice yourself stressed or with something out of the norm within your physical form, you can step up and wake up into the embodiment of an extraordinary life.

Through resting instead of stressing, bringing your past to conscious conclusions, befriending your body and feelings, clearing conflict and embodying positive virtues, you have a recipe for radiant health. You've been blessed with a body and it wants you to use it for a fulfilled life. It is my hope that Body Calm offers a regular reminder to remain consciously calm, rediscover holistic harmony and live every moment fully and completely from the love-filled home of your own heart.

Rest is Best + Harmony Heals.

Next Steps

KEEPING CALM

ACADEMY

If you would like to learn and benefit from Body Calm and/or Mind Calm and get qualified to share these transformational techniques with others, then check out Sandy's Calm Academy. It offers web-based home-study courses that you access from anywhere in the world, and you will get the care and attention you need along the way by working with your own trainer via Skype. Millions of people crave more calm in their lives and are waiting to learn meditation from you! As an added bonus, you can make a bigger, positive difference by also joining Sandy's team of trainers. So study at home and change the world by visiting www.thecalmacademy.com

RETREATS

Sandy runs Calm Retreats in the UK and abroad for mind, body and soul. During a long weekend in the UK or a week's retreat at one of his international venues, you will have the opportunity to learn meditation from Sandy and his team, and so deepen your experience using the techniques. For more information, visit www.mindbodyco.co.uk

COACHING

Work with Sandy one-to-one over a series of Skype sessions to experience Mind Calm and Body Calm. For more information, visit www.sandynewbigging.com. If you'd like to work with a Body Calm Coach who Sandy has trained, visit www.thecalmacademy.com and look in the Trainer Bio's section, then get in touch via the Contact Us form.

GUIDED SELF-HEALING MEDITATIONS

Sandy has recorded a series of guided meditations based upon the Body Calm Directories, that can help you to heal the mind-based causes of specific conditions. Please visit www.sandynewbigging.com for audio track listings and to download them.

MIND CALM

Sandy's other technique is called Mind Calm and is the modern-day meditation technique that gives you 'peace with mind'. If you've enjoyed *Body Calm*, you will love *Mind Calm*! For more information, visit www.sandynewbigging.com where you can subscribe to his newsletter, get access to two chapters from Mind Calm and two of the tracks from his bestselling album.

REFERENCES

Introduction – Helping Your Body to Heal

1. http://www.bbc.co.uk/news/health-30411246; accessed 31 May 2015

2. http://www.telegraph.co.uk/news/health/11259122/NHS-spends-on-80-million-a-year-on-paracetamol-prescriptions.html; accessed 31 May 2015

3. http://www.bbc.co.uk/news/health-30411246; accessed 31 May 2015

Chapter 2 – Big Benefits of Body Calm

1. http://www.ncbi.nlm.nih.gov/pubmed/21035949; accessed 31 May 2015

2. http://www.ncbi.nlm.nih.gov/pubmed/22569185; accessed 31 May 2015

3. Dusek JA, Otu HH, Wohlhueter AL, Bhasin M, Zerbini LF, Joseph MG, et al. (2008) Genomic Counter-Stress Changes Induced by the Relaxation Response. PLoS ONE 3(7): e2576. doi:10.1371/journal.pone.0002576

4. http://www.ncbi.nlm.nih.gov/pubmed/25566158; accessed 31 May 2015

5. http://www.ncbi.nlm.nih.gov/pubmed/25509967; accessed 31 May 2015

6. http://www.ncbi.nlm.nih.gov/pubmed/25041058; accessed 31 May 2015

7. Carlson, L. E., Beattie, T. L., Giese-Davis, J., Faris, P., Tamagawa, R., Fick, L. J., Degelman, E. S. and Speca, M. (2015), Mindfulness-based cancer recovery and supportive-expressive therapy maintain telomere length relative to controls in distressed breast cancer survivors. Cancer, 121: 476–484. doi: 10.1002/cncr.29063

8. http://www.ncbi.nlm.nih.gov/pubmed/25537522; accessed 31 May 2015

9. http://www.ncbi.nlm.nih.gov/pubmed/25711654; accessed 31 May 2015

10. http://www.ncbi.nlm.nih.gov/pubmed/25686304; accessed 31 May 2015

11. http://www.ncbi.nlm.nih.gov/pubmed/25142566; accessed 31 May 2015

12. http://www.ncbi.nlm.nih.gov/pubmed/25613595; accessed 31 May 2015

13. http://www.ncbi.nlm.nih.gov/pubmed/25673114; accessed 31 May 2015

14. http://www.ncbi.nlm.nih.gov/pubmed/25598736; accessed 31 May 2015

15. http://www.ncbi.nlm.nih.gov/pubmed/25620166; accessed 31 May 2015

16. http://www.ncbi.nlm.nih.gov/pubmed/25425224; accessed 31 May 2015

17. http://www.ncbi.nlm.nih.gov/pubmed/25105026; accessed 31 May 2015

18. http://www.ncbi.nlm.nih.gov/pubmed/25035626; accessed 31 May 2015

Chapter 3 – Stop Stressing and Start Resting

1. http://news.harvard.edu/gazette/story/2010/11/wandering-mind-not-a-happy-mind; accessed 5 June 2015

Chapter 11 – Unloved Body

1. https://www.heartmath.org/research/research-library/basic/physiological-and-psychological-effects-of-compassion-and-anger-01/; accessed 15 June 2015

2. Hamilton, D. *Why Kindness is Good for You* (Hay House, 2010)

ABOUT THE AUTHOR

Sandy C. Newbigging is the creator of the Mind Detox Method and Mind Calm and Body Calm Meditation techniques. He has written several bestselling books including *Heal the Hidden Cause*, *Life Detox*, *New Beginnings*, *Thunk!* and *Mind Calm*. This work has been seen on a number of TV channels including Discovery Health. Sandy is available for consultations via Skype, he also runs mind–body–soul residential retreats, and trains Mind Detox, Mind Calm and Body Calm coaches via his award-winning Calm Academy.

He was recently commended by the Federation of Holistic Therapists as Tutor of the Year, and has been described by Yoga magazine as 'one of the best meditation teachers around'. For more information and workshops by Sandy C. Newbigging or to book him for a speaking event, please use the following contact details:

 answers@sandynewbigging.com

 minddetoxman

 sandynewbigging

 sandynewbigging.tumblr.com

www.sandynewbigging.com